W9-DDK-067

Poetry with Some Flowers, Birds and Teddy Bears

Poetry with Some Flowers, Birds and Teddy Bears

Inspirational, Romance, and Life

Original Poems and Photography by Robert J Lessig
Bird Illustrations by Ronald R Lessig

8/08/04

Kerie,

What a voice!

God bless you.
you're the best!

Bob Lessig
+ Linda

Published by **BRW**
Fleetwood, Pennsylvania

Copyright © 2001 by Robert J. Lessig
Bird illustrations by Ronald R. Lessig

All rights reserved. No part of this book may be reproduced or transmitted in any form or by any means, electronic or mechanical, including photocopying, recording, or by any information storage and retrieval system, without permission in writing from the publisher.

Extracts from the Authorized Version of the Bible (The King James Bible), the rights in which are vested in the Crown, are reproduced by permission of the Crown's Patentee, Cambridge University Press.

Published by BIBLICAL RESEARCH WRITINGS
237 E. Main Street
Fleetwood, PA 19522-1414

Publisher's Cataloging-in-Publication Data
Lessig, Robert J.
    Poetry with some flowers, birds and teddy bears: inspirational, romance, and life / Robert J. Lessig — Fleetwood, PA : Biblical Research Writings, 2001.
        p.   ill.   cm.
    ISBN 0-9667763-0-5

    1. Inspiration—Poetry.   2. Christian life—Poetry.   I. Title.
PS3562.E875 P64   2001   00-104494
811 .54   dc—21   CIP

PROJECT COORDINATION BY JENKINS GROUP, INC.

04   03   02   01   00   x*   5   4   3   2   1

Printed in China

This book of poetry with flowers, and birds, and teddy bears is dedicated to Linda, my wonderful wife, whose beauty inspired me, whose love encouraged me, and whose strength motivated me.

the author

the artist

Contents

∿ INSPIRATIONAL ∿

SECTION I — FLOWERS

SECTION II — BIRDS

Contents

❧ ROMANCE & LIFE ☙

SECTION III — TEDDY BEARS

Foreword

Robert Lessig has created a wonderful volume of poetry replete with his original photographs of flowers and teddy bears, plus his brother Ron's watercolor bird illustrations. Knowing that these poems and pictures are dedicated to his wife, Linda, deepens the poignancy of his poetic flights.

Robert's spiritual soarings take us into our own souls, motivating us to examine human destiny in new ways. His spiritual espousals deepen our own spiritual visions and aspirations. His love of nature and of human nature—especially for his wife—is admirable, and his sensitivity for his loved ones is expressed with incisive sentiment—never broaching sentimentality.

Especially notable for their poetic artistry and poignant emotion are the following poems—my favorites: "Called to be Saints," "The Voices of the Seasons," "What is Man?," "Beauty," "And Then There Is This," and "A World Unknown." Which poems are your favorites?

We readers of this volume of poetry will be enriched, enlightened and enraptured. Rereading these poems will fill our days with joy.

— Charles J. Scanzello, Professor Emeritus
Kutztown University
Kutztown, Pennsylvania

Linda and Bob

Acknowledgments

A special thank you to those great men of God from Ohio who taught me the inherent and inerrant accuracy and integrity of the Word of God which form the foundation for the poetry in this volume.

I would also like to give credit to those at the Jenkins Group who worked so hard on this book to turn it into an exquisite volume of poetry: Eric Norton, Theresa Nelson, Nikki Stahl and Tom White.

Introduction

This book of poetry consists of three sections. Sections I and II contain inspirational poetry which will help you to understand biblical truths in greater detail. Faith, love, hope, the believer's responsibility to God and many other subjects are written about with clarity and focus on God's heart, intent and purposes in His Word. You will see man taken from the depths of despair to victory in the greatness of the high and noble calling of what God has made him to be in Christ.

Section III contains poetry about living life. There is romance, adventure, humor and observations about life which will entertain you, and perhaps make you smile.

The photos of beautiful flowers in Section I, the drawings of birds in Section II, and the photos of teddy bears in Section III will soothe your soul, bless your heart, and ease your mind.

May this volume of poetry inspire you, energize you, and help you build your believing, trust, and confidence in God and His magnificent Word.

Inspirational
SECTION I

Poetry
and Some Beautiful Flowers

The Voices of the Seasons

The cold winds of winter howl aloud, and in restless
    rhythms sing,
And the earth is still, and the land lays bare of the life
    that it has seen.
The meadows and valleys of the countryside, and
    hills and mountains show,
Their new found beauty as they soon put on, white
    faces of new fallen snow.

The sweet melodies of Spring's vibrant voice, are
    heard midst the forests' green leaves,
And the fields, and gardens obey its command, and
    the fruit and flower bring.
The rain comes almost daily now, falling steadily,
    sometimes with passion.
The robin has returned in triumphant flight, and
    butterflies in spectacular fashion.

Summer whispers, and its breath ushers in, warm and
    sun-filled days.
It patiently welcomes and prepares fall's harvest, of
    golden corn, and wheat, and hay.
And the seed beneath the fertile soil replies, tho not in
    any particular hurry,
For the days are long, there is time to grow, mother
    nature knows no worry.

Autumn echoes all autumns past, as scenic vistas
    explode with a view.
Colorful pigments and hues so brilliant, radiantly
    appear because they're now due.
And the grass of lawns, and flowers of fields, and
    forests where tall trees stand,
All are changed, and are not the same, their displays
    of great splendor enhanced.

I pause for a moment of time now and then, to
    consider, to hear, to listen,
To these voices so clear, and plain, but distinct,
    because each boasts of its very own season.
And I am grateful to God, for He determined the
    days, He set the times, and the hours,
Of Spring, and Summer, and Winter and Autumn,
    with His great hand and with His mighty power.

What is Man?

"What is man," the psalmist asks, "that thou art
    mindful of him?"
For He does indeed know each of us, and searches the
    hearts of all men.
He created the heavens for earth, the earth for man,
    and man for Himself above,
And then chose each one to faithfully come, to stand
    before Him in love.

"What is man," the psalmist asks, "for thou hast made
    him little lower than the angels?"
God gave him His spirit, creating him in His image,
    in His presence he may peacefully dwell.
Of the dust of the earth his body He formed, made his
    soul alive with His breath,
And gave him power and dominion o'er all the earth,
    and man was truly blessed.

"What is man," the psalmist asks, "that thou has
    crowned him with glory and honor?"
He's strong in His might, standing fast in the fight,
    his enemies scattered asunder.
He walks tall and proud, clothed in the armour of
    God, as he lives a life of obedience.
His loins are girded, his feet are shod, his heart
    willing and filled with believing.

Now God had a plan when He made man, and
    formed, and created He him,
For He knew that man would soon disobey, and that
    he would eventually sin.
And for the world He so loved, that His will would be
    done, He sent His only begotten Son,
That whosoever would chose, his life wouldn't lose,
    He called His plan Salvation.

We've been redeemed, we've been justified,
    sanctified and made righteous, from all of sin's
    bondage we're free.
Once earthern vessels, we are now priceless treasures,
    to the praise of God's glory we'll be.
For He is mindful of us, and has made all of us just a
    little lower than the angels.
And we are His masterpiece, created in Christ,
    endued with His mighty power, living in grace,
    His mercy and peace, and crowned with His
    glory and honor.

Faith

[Our God-given Ability]

Faith is the spiritual ability we receive,
  when we are born again of incorruptible seed.

It is not blind as some may say,
  that we need not know anything to find our
  way.

For it is based in the Word which we study to know,
  to find His direction on which way to go.

Do we take a "step" of faith without knowledge or
  wisdom
  to light our way when we make a decision?

No! The Word lights our way so we won't stumble
  along;
  each "step" we take guided, both sure and
  strong.

Faith is the ability given to all Christians by God,
  everyone receives, no one is left out,

But, does God give to some men more faith than
  others,
  like men of renown known the whole world
  over?

And, can I get more faith if I don't have enough
  to get through the day when the going gets
  tough?

The amount of faith He gives is always the same
  measure,
  no one gets more, no one has less, ever!

The law was our schoolmaster before faith came;
  it was weak in the flesh, so it was replaced
  by the faith of Jesus Christ, at Pentecost, with
  grace.

Now we can move mountains,
  this is not a brag nor boast,

For this faith of Christ is our God-given ability
  to believe God to the uttermost.

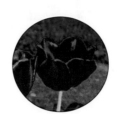

Behold the Glory

Behold the glory of God in your life,
His will accomplished, what a magnificent sight.
His Word believed, the spirit energized,
His power manifested as you walk in the light.
His manifold wisdom that He freely imparts,
guides your reason and counsels your heart.
His peace, His strength, His prosperity abound,
more precious than silver, and gold easily found.

Behold the glory of the Lord today,
for you are what God says you are:
His masterpiece created in Christ
righteous, redeemed and set apart.
Behold the glory of the Lord today,
for you can do what He says you can do:
endued with power from up on high,
it is Christ who strengtheneth you.
Behold the glory of the Lord today,
for you have what God says you have:
an inheritance as a joint heir with Christ
and all spiritual blessings in abundant supply.
Behold the glory of the Lord today,
for you will be what He says you will be:
victorious in life, peaceful inside,
and His son through eternity.

Seed

A fellow laborer sowed a seed one time,
    (he worked for the Lord, you know).
With love in his heart, he broadcast with joy
    knowing he would reap what he would sow.
With his hand to the plow, and not looking back,
    he diligently tilled each furrow.
And he rejoiced at the fertile soil he'd found
    no thorns, no tares, no barren, stony ground.

Like Paul, and Apollos, who planted and watered,
    he sowed God's Word of hope and grace
Deep within the hearts and minds of believing men,
    who soon became rooted and grounded in faith.
I listened as he spoke of the plenteous harvest,
    and of fruit, and of the vine, and the branches.
And of the Promised Seed he spoke eloquently,
    Christ, conceived by the virgin Mary.

I marvelled at the beauty of each grain of truth
    he sowed with boldness and love.
He told of the incorruptible seed God sent,
    on the day of Pentecost, from above.
How God saved our souls, and made us whole,
    it was truly a remarkable story,
That we are born again of His spiritual seed:
    "Christ in you, the hope of glory."

Redeemed and Walking

There was a time, many long years ago,
    in days that have long since passed.
I remember feeling like a weary stranger,
    like a foreigner in a foreign land.
I was tossed to-and-fro, didn't know which way to go,
    got real tired of being deceived.
I was ever learning, but never knowing or coming
    to the truth that could set me free.

I felt weak and unworthy as I was blown about,
    heeding fables, and other doctrine.
My conversation was with those who did not know,
    with those who were so disobedient.
I swerved aside and heard vain janglings
    such as I could not even perceive.
But, I yearned to be righteous, not wise in my own eyes,
    and it was then that God rescued me.

NOW,
IN THIS DAY, IN THIS TIME, IN THIS HOUR I AM

No longer a stranger, a foreigner lost,
    I am rooted, and grounded in God's wonderful
    love.
No longer forever being tossed, to-and-fro,
    I am standing fast in liberty, and standing bold.
No longer blown about with every wind of doctrine,
    but I am running the race, and I'm assured of
    winning.
No longer heeding fables and believing such,
    my eyes are enlightened, and I'm strong in the
    Lord.
No longer unworthy, or helpless, or weak,
    I am walking by the spirit with which God
    redeemed me.

God's Magnificent Word

When I read God's Magnificent Word,
my heart is thrilled inside.
I read about what He's done for me,
how He sent His Son to die.
And I thank my God, my heavenly Father,
whose gift in me resides.
He's made me one of His own,
to me His will He made known,
His truth I cannot, I will not deny.

I wake up each morning to a brand new day,
so thankful to be alive.
Because I study His Word and know His will,
I'll be sure to rightly decide
What to do each moment,
believing trusting His wisdom,
His spirit in me energized.
I'm never alone, never on my own,
as I live the more abundant life.

What Is It Then

What is it then, that you expect God to do,
    about all of the problems each day facing you?
For He's given *you* power to defeat and conquer,
    it's the *power* of Christ within.
Triumph and victory is your way of life,
    as a Christian it is your goal to win.
Filled with His spirit, strengthened with His might,
    you're ready for the race to run, stand or fight.

What is it then, that God expects you to do,
    about all of the problems He sees facing you?
You continually pray for what He's already given,
    all things pertaining to godliness and living.
All the while struggling and striving and stumbling,
    overwhelmed daily by life's many challenges.
Your ability to overcome lies dormant within,
    while you wait for God, to do what *He* can.

What is it then, you are going to do,
    about all the problems each day facing you?
Changing your mind, and making decisions
    based on His Word about life and living.
Doubts and worries you boldly cast aside,
    daily taking charge, doing what you know is right.
Your prayers He hears, and to them He surely listens,
    but it's your believing, and your actions, that get
    His attention.

Live for God: always doing what is right.

Live by God: using His power, strength and might.

Live in God: walking in fellowship, your mind renewed.

Live with God: constantly knowing His power and presence are always in you and with you.

Inspirational
SECTION II

Poetry
and Some Delightful Birds

Set Free

Where are you God? My heart is despairing, and I
    really need to know.
The road is hard, I've a heavy load, and there's still a
    long way to go.
My body is tired, my soul is weary, and my spirit is
    languished within.
I need your help to stay a course, for I've no strength
    to keep wandering.

Are you listening God, do you hear my call? I really
    need to know.
Each step I take, each mile I go, I hope will soon take
    me home.
Oh how I hope for the day when my journey shall
    end, perhaps it will be on the morrow,
Then I will have peace, there'll be time to rest, and I
    will no longer sorrow.

Can you see me God, will you answer my prayer? I
really need to know.

I've gotten lost somehow along my way, the days are
sad and uncertain.

Guilt, and shame, and pride and fear have been my
steady companions.

Will you forgive, and let me live? Will you free me
from sin and its bondage?

Do you hear me child? I love you son, I really want
you to know.

I've heard your call, your despair I know, and surely
your prayer I've answered.

My Word is a lamp unto your feet, my Son has blazed
a trail of believing.

Your way home is clear; He's taken your burdens;
you've been set free in your body, your soul, and
your spirit.

In God's Family

O' that now are we sons of God,
   born again of His spirit, when we confessed Jesus
   as Lord.

Endeared by His grace, His mercy, and love,
   He so lavishly bestowed upon each of our souls,

The eyes of our understanding being enlightened, we
   know,
   because we ask for wisdom, He gives to us
   liberally, and we grow,

In a household of glory, where angels stand,
   we're seated together in Christ, at God's own right
   hand.

O' to be redeemed from the wicked course of this
  world,
  chosen by Him, and set apart, to be one of the
  fold.
We walk worthy of the vocation wherewith we are
  called,
  fellow laborers with Him, we know we can't fail.
Searching the Scriptures daily, studying to show
  ourselves approved,
  believing what is written, believing what is truth.
We study to know the Bible, to understand, then
  believe, then act,
  taking control of our lives as we do so, to
  demonstrate our faith.

O' to be filled with the spirit of power, and of God's
  unfailing love,
  and a sound mind never fearing, but standing fast
  and bold.

We stir up this spirit within us, putting on the Word in
  our minds,
  its presence manifested, a light that brightly shines.

We make His Word our own and we hide it in our hearts,
  to counsel us and guide us, each day a brand new
  start.

Once dead in sins, now made alive, once weak in the
  flesh, now strong,
  He made us worthy, He delivered us, to His family
  we belong.

The Gift

Have you read in the Bible the wonderful story
    about "Christ in you, the hope of glory?"
Of the "riches of the mystery" that God had kept
    hidden from men and from angels from the very
    beginning?
The day of Pentecost had been a long time coming;
    it was the day God chose for the original
    outpouring
Of the gift of holy spirit whereby we call,
    "Abba Father."
We are born again, and as His sons,
    we've been endued with its mighty power.

You and I have Christ in us, and are completely,
    complete in Him.
So, we take a stand, and fight the good fight,
    knowing we will always win.
Doubts, and worries, and fears and woes
    may trouble us every day.
But, greater is He that is in us,
    so we can make them go away.

God doesn't care what we used to be,
    He doesn't care what we've done.
He only cares what we want to do,
    what we are willing to become!
So what are you going to do with the "Christ in you,"
    —the gift of holy spirit that God's freely given?
Will your life as God's son be pleasing to Him,
    and, will it show in your daily living?

Mercy

Who among us can comprehend
the abundant mercy with which God redeemed man?
How much more merciful could He have been,
than to rescue us all from our mortal sin;
The consequences for which Christ paid the price
when he died on Calvary, giving us eternal life?
How much more mercy, at how great a cost,
nailing your sins and mine to Calvary's cross?

Because of God's mercy (on account of His love),
we now live in **grace** as we *walk, stand or run.*
His *only* begotten Son He sacrificed for the world,
for He loved us down to a man.
He saved our souls and made us whole, it was part of
His salvation plan.

Because of God's mercy, we are His sons with power,
living by believing Him each day, every hour.
How much more mercy, then, do you think we need,
to live the more abundant life He gave to you and me?
You see, it is not more mercy
that we need in our lives,
His grace wherein we stand is sufficient.
When we pray to God
we need only ask for and receive
His tremendous, ever present forgiveness.

Believing In, and Believing Him

You tell me you believe in God, my friend,
    and I am glad to hear that you do.
But believing in God is not enough, you know,
    you must also believe what He's written to you.
The thoughts, and ideas and opinions you harbour
    on what life is all about,
Though they contradict what God clearly tells you,
    do you trust in them anyhow?
He magnified His Word above all His name,
    to make it easy for you to know.
You must rightly divide it to understand it and live it,
    speaking the truth in love as you grow.

You tell me you believe in God, my friend,
    and I'm glad to hear that you do.
But do you have confidence in, and trust His Word,
    believing His wisdom will carry you through?
Do you live in fear from day to day,
    doubting what life may eventually bring?
Or do you trust in God, your fear cast out
    by the mature love spoken of by Him?
Are you worried, or troubled, or do you fret,
    your mind in turmoil and oft times upset?
God wants your heart, His Word always believing,
    your trust, and confidence,
        your loyalty, and allegiance.

Called To Be Saints

Does not our heart burn within us
    when you and I hear the Word of our Lord?
And our passion not grow in the fire's fierce glow,
    its flames consuming the chaff in our soul?
Knowing no power on earth can withstand the man,
    who's committed to God and His Word,
We go, stand and speak to all the world's people
    the truth that we have so eagerly learned.

Are our days not brightened, and our minds enlightened
    as we thrive with His wisdom, and love?
Once deceived by the flesh, once blinded by lusts,
    are we not now renewed, and righteous and strong?
His peace abounding and His grace surrounding,
    we're redeemed, and no longer dead in sin.
Called to be saints, we now live as God's sons,
    sanctified by the "new man" within.

The Night

☾

Venus waltzes with the moon in a bright and star-
   filled sky,
The hoot owl sings his lonely song in the stillness of
   the night.
Tall trees parade along the banks, in step with the
   winding river,
They keep their ranks as they march in time with its
   harmony and rythym.

The mountains stand like faithful sentinels, true
   guardians of places high,
They await the messengers of the morning sun, bright
   beams that bring warmth and light.
Alone, I hear and see nature's wonders, in the
   darkness of the hour,
But not so dark that I cannot see, it's by God's
   handiwork and His mighty power.

Viewpoint

Have you ever stopped, or taken the time
— you know, just a moment or two,
To consider a situation, a problem or circumstance,
from another's point of view?
What a truly remarkable sight you might see,
what treasures of truth you could learn,
If you put on hold your own thoughts and opinion,
and listen while the other fellow takes his turn.

Your understanding may be increased,
and your knowledge and wisdom grow.
You'll be amazed at how much more there is
when you hear what the other fellow knows.
You may be right, or you may be wrong
with your logic, and reasoning and thinking,
But what a tremendous blessing and surprise is yours,
if his advice keeps your ship from sinking.

How humbling it is of mind and heart
and how thrilling it is to find,
That there is a better way that's not our own,
shown to us by someone kind.

Romance & Life

Poetry and
Some Wonderful Teddy Bears

Beauty

Life At Home

A Kiss, A Hug, A Smile

Living Life

And Then There Is This

It's Not Easy Being You

A World Unknown

Beauty

I've seen the multicolored hues of the Northern Lights
    displayed,
Their beams of light filling the dark night sky in
    mystical array.
They would shimmer, and dance, and twist and shine
    amidst the moon and stars.
How beautiful, how beautiful, I thought that they all are.

I've seen the rugged mountains with their snow
    capped peaks so high,
And admired them in awe from their summits I had
    climbed.
They zigged, and zagged for miles on end in majestic
    ease and grace.
How beautiful, how beautiful, I thought of this, their
    place.

I've watched in the early morning hours the rising of
the sun,
And viewed with delight it painting the sky before the
day'd begun.
It spread its colors far and wide on the horizon I
could see.
How beautiful, how beautiful, I thought the dawning
of the day to be.

I've watched the pounding surf of the ocean blue and
deep,
And listened to its peaceful voice before I'd go to
sleep.
It's rythym held so steady as the tide came in and out.
How beautiful, how beautiful, I thought its sight and
sound.

Yes, all the beauty that I've seen, and heard about and
learned,
All filled and satisfied me with treasures I've not
earned.
And all of these are truly great, and have very much
blessed my life,
But none has thrilled my heart, nor stirred my soul
as Linda, a woman, my friend, my wife.

Life At Home

What if anger was not allowed
in your home to be displayed?
Nor show of force to intimidate,
or actions in fear that strike out in hate?
Nor loudness of voice, or screams, or shouts,
to quench the spirit of those about?
What if instead of anger and rage,
which tear apart, and hurt, and maim,
You replaced them all and made up your mind,
to let peace and love rule your heart every time?
With quiet, and calm, and words softly spoken,
on lips of a soul filled with tenderness often,
Gone would be the pain and the sorrow,
of lives that are hurt by pride, and longing.
And spirits once quenched and badly broken,
restored now, and strong, by love's
many kind tokens.

A Kiss, A Hug, A Smile

My favorite time of day occurs,
in the early morning hours,
When she greets me with a tender kiss,
a warm hug, and a smile.
And when I hug her back,
and kiss her on the cheek,
She holds me closer still, and softly
whispers "I love you" tenderly.
As we hold each other in gentle embrace
for just a moment or two,
I think about our lives together,
our hearts entwined, our souls are one,
And how the promises we made are true,
It's a great day, and it's only just begun!

Living Life

Exciting, enjoyable, escapades entangled,
Emotions run wild, the passions unbridled.
Romance and adventure, sometimes regrettable,
but never to this day forgettable.
Yesteryear, yesterday, playgrounds of the soul,
Seemed like fun forever, even amidst the turmoil.

The ride of a lifetime once so sought after,
Crashed and burned, I can still hear the laughter.
Exploits explosive, taking it to the wall,
Pushing the envelope, a very close call.

Ship not coming in, bridges burned every mile,
Road blocks ahead, and up hill battles,
Success elusive, so too, fortune and fame,
Losing, as well as winning, was part of the game.

Now putting off old and worn out fashions,
Perceiving newer, nonconforming visions.
A different fire burns fiercely now,
Thoughts now captive, not uncontrolled.
Renewed, made stronger, with life giving wisdom,
Pressing toward the mark of a higher calling.

And Then There Is This

There was a crooked man who walked a crooked
 mile.
I heard this rhyme a thousand times when I was but a
 child.
Seems everything in this man's life was a little less
 than great.
One day he hollered these now famous words, "Now
 let's get one thing straight."

And then there is this:
Grandpa always liked to rise in the early morning
 hours,
To watch the sun come over the hill, to see if there
 were showers.
Looking out the window for a little while he'd turn
 slowly to Grandma and say,
"Well, my dear we best get up. Yes, it looks like
 another day."

And then there is this:
The CEO decided to have a meeting of all the
    company's staff.
Seems like rules were being broken in his opaque
    glass manufacturing plant.
The time for fixing things he knew was drawing near
"Now listen men," he calmly stated, "and let me
    make this perfectly clear."

And then there is this:
The centepede now fully grown had come into his
    own,
He confidently decided it was time for him to leave
    his home.
He dressed his best from head to toe, he was a perfect
    vision
But he soon learned how tough it was to make his
    first decision.
His mother's words he'd remember then, and surely
    long there after.
"Now son," she said, "Be sure to always put your best
    foot forward."

It's Not Easy Being You

Have you ever noticed when you get ahead of yourself
    you really wind up behind?
And soon you find that you're beside yourself,
    and have trouble making up your mind.
Running around in circles,
    you try to square things away.
And as you tie up loose ends you soon reach the end
    of your rope, now worn and frayed.

Trying to straighten things out gets you all bent
    out of shape,
    so you draw the line but "they" cross it anyway.
So you throw your hands up in the air in despair
    but then find it hard to grasp anything
And putting your foot down firmly,
    you find it difficult to take further steps again.
And now you're ticked off because it's getting late
    and you lost all sense of time.
You'll be glad to go to bed,
    but know you'll just twist and turn,
        as you slowly try to unwind.

A World Unknown

My heart filled with great excitement when I looked
    into her eyes,
For I beheld a world I'd never known, a world there
    deep inside.
She stood before me smiling sweetly, as my spirit
    soared within,
And my soul took flight to greater heights than it had
    ever been.

I saw wonderful promises to be kept, in the joy of two
    lives shared,
There was grace, and beauty, and kindness too, and
    wisdom was not spared,
And fun and hope and love untold, and strength in
    hearts that bonded.
Oh how I thrilled at the sight, this beautiful sight as I
    entered in undaunted.

For a moment I was lost in time when she beckoned
    me, "Come along,"
And I had no fear of being there, her voice
    comforting as a song.
I boldly took her hand in mine as we strolled down
    peaceful paths,
And I began to see, and know this world I'd found,
    and I was very glad.

I guard my heart most carefully now, for with
    treasures it is filled,
Though I've taken nothing from this world, it
    overflows, and won't be still.
For this woman in whose eyes I saw, and beheld a
    whole new life,
I asked, and she accepted, and agreed to become my
    wife.

Order Information

You may purchase additional copies of *Poetry With Some Flowers, Birds, and Teddy Bears* at your bookstore or order from us direct. Please fill out this handy coupon and send it along with your check or money order (made payable to BRW) to:

BRW
237 East Main Street
Fleetwood, PA 19522-1414

Name:_____

Address: _____

City: ___ _____State: _____Zip: _____

Please send me _____ copy(s) @ $17.95 each.

I am enclosing $_____

plus Postage and Handling* $_____

Sales Tax (where applicable) $_____

Total amount enclosed $_____

*Add $4 for the first book and $1 for each additional book.

Prices are subject to change without notice.

Kit 'n Kat

The Nose Knows

S0-AXX-442

Kit 'n Kat
The Nose Knows

Linda Felton Steinbaum
Carly Alison Steinbaum

www.mascotbooks.com

Kit 'n Kat: The Nose Knows

©2019 Linda Felton Steinbaum and Carly Alison Steinbaum.
All Rights Reserved. No part of this publication may be
reproduced, stored in a retrieval system or transmitted
in any form by any means electronic, mechanical, or
photocopying, recording or otherwise without the permission
of the author.

For more information, please contact:
Mascot Books
620 Herndon Parkway, Suite 320
Herndon, VA 20170
info@mascotbooks.com

Library of Congress Control Number: 2018910485

CPSIA Code: PRFRE0219A
ISBN-13: 978-1-64307-108-4

Printed in Canada

For Biscuit

Chapter 1

"Well, butter my butt and call me a biscuit!" Mom shrieked into the phone from the kitchen.

Thanks for that, Mom. I was relaxing on the sofa and totally absorbed in my latest crime novel until her shrill voice took me out of the moment. How irritating and thoughtless. Not to mention I had to hear that stupid phrase again. Mom saves that dumb expression for when something really shocks her. That "gem" was passed down to her from her Southern mother. Too bad Nana's recipe for bread pudding wasn't passed down instead. I don't really understand what it means, but when I shared it with Evie, she just laughed and told me sometimes her great aunt calls out, "Hot pot of coffee!" Okay. That's goofy too. You see, sense of humor is one reason Evie and I are best friends.

But even though we're really close, we're not connected at the hip like some of the popular girls at school. We have a few different interests and hang out with other people sometimes. That's fine. For example, she likes to shop and I don't. So she does that with Laurel. And Evie isn't into drones like Jack and I are. Jack is my other best friend. His parents are divorced, and he lives with his dad. We would always hang out on Sundays when it was a nice day. He's very smart and likes science like I do. Last year, he built a winding obstacle course through the trees for us to test our drone skills. It came in handy on Halloween. We put little sheets and faces over our drones and flew them outside my front door when kids came to trick-or-treat. It was great scaring everybody.

But getting back to the point. I thought, *Wow, what could have shocked Mom so much on this calm, quiet Saturday?* But whatever, I decided to continue reading. Because really, what could anyone tell her that could be so interesting? Obviously nothing half as intriguing as this book I was reading. And I was just getting to the part where I thought the crime was going to be solved. Mom's drama would just have to wait. I wanted to find out "whodunit."

But then I heard Mom do one of her big, silly, singsong sighs. She only makes that delightful sound when she's really, really surprised. And then her eyes bug out, and she clutches her chest like she's having a heart attack. Not a pretty picture. But that made me distracted, so I put my book down to investigate.

The one fact I knew was that she was talking to Mark. You don't have to be Sherlock Holmes to guess that one. Lots of clues there. First, she smiles a lot and flutters her eyelashes. And then her voice gets a little higher and she giggles. Kind of sickening. Oh, Mark. Did I tell you about him? Mark is my mother's new husband. And he's very annoying. But I'll get to that later.

Meanwhile, I wondered what Mark could have possibly said that would get Mom so worked up. Well, I found out soon after, and *hot pot of coffee*! It was in that little phone call that Mark gave her the news that would ruin my life.

Not kidding. He had announced that he got a promotion at work, and his boss wanted to transfer him to a bigger office in another state. And there just happened to be a big, beautiful house available for us there. That morning, they had showed Mark pictures, and he loved it. He told his boss that his wife would have to okay the move and the house. But apparently Mom said okay without even looking at the photographs. Now did anyone consult me about this life changer? I don't think so. How insulting. I was just simply informed we were going to pick up and move. Butter my butt and call me miserable.

I should have seen this disaster coming, but I had thought things couldn't get any worse than when Mom started dating Mark. She had met him at her yoga class. Apparently, he had lost a football bet at work and had to put on yoga pants and go to a hot yoga class, where they turn the temperature up really high and everyone sweats. How lucky for me that he signed up for her class. She told me she thought he looked cute in his tight little outfit and that they had smiled at each other before class. I only wish it had stopped at that. But no, the yoga gods weren't on my side this time.

Apparently, Mark took his place right in back of Mom. While doing the stretches and poses, he tried to copy what she was doing until he nearly fainted from the heat and had to be carried out before *shavasana*—the ending rest pose. Mom was concerned and rushed to get him some cold water. And the rest is history. A heartbreaking history, I might add. Soon after that class, they started going out to dinner once or twice a week. And then, to my horror, she starting inviting him over for dinner on Sundays, cutting my drone time with Jack short. And those dinners were so uncomfortable. Mark smiled too big and always tried to tell jokes. And he wasn't funny. And he was loud. And he chewed with his mouth open, and sometimes food would fly out. One time a mushy piece of carrot landed on my arm. I can honestly say that because of hot yoga, my nice, peaceful life had come to a cruel end. Thanks and *namaste*.

"You know I really like him, Katherine," she told me one day after she and Mark had been dating about six months. "And our signs are very compatible."

She never calls me Katherine. That was my clue that I didn't want to hear any more of this conversation. And I was right. It was then that Mom announced to me that she and Mark were going to get married. Does that mean I would have a new dad?

Of course I want Mom to be happy, and not that Mark is a terrible person, but I already have a dad. Or at least I had a dad. Sadly, he got cancer and died before my fourth birthday. But I don't want another one. I was used to it being just Mom and me. And we've done okay. Sure, we weren't able to do fancy things, and a few times Mom couldn't pay the electric bill, but she acted like that was a great experience.

"This is so spiritual, Kat. Who needs artificial light?" she had assured me as she lit candles. For the record, I didn't fall for that one. My friends think Mom is an old hippie because, among other things, she wears lots of jewelry and beads, is a health food nut, loves yoga stuff, and sells Native American artifacts. And maybe she is a little different, and sometimes wacky even, but I love her.

So after she made that dreadful announcement, one night out of some sense of loyalty, I decided to look at old videos to try to remember life with my real dad. Mom kept them in a file on her computer. She didn't know I could see them, but she only has one password—meditate—so this was pretty easy to find. It was a strange feeling. On the screen he seemed so alive as he threw me up in the air and twirled me around. And I watched as he sung lullabies at bedtime. He had such a beautiful, soothing singing voice...that of course I didn't inherit. I think all I got from him were his green eyes and big ears. And maybe some of his engineering skills. I say this because Jack called me a genius that time I helped figure out how to build our first drone. Jack knew all the terminology and got all the materials, but after we both built the frame, I figured out what pieces were put on wrong. That was why our drone had been vibrating.

Anyway, unbelievably, Mark would now be in our family videos. Hey, he's a nice guy, and might not be so bad as someone else's dad, but I knew the minute I had a meal with him, I had no interest in having him around. Jack and Evie reminded me he slips me some cash sometimes, he bought me a new phone, and took us all to the movies a few times. But I don't care. He is big and clumsy and takes up too much space. And everything he does is too loud. His laugh is boisterous, his sneeze is deafening, and he even claps his hands during a ball game thunderously. It's beyond annoying. Not to also point out that it's because of him we had to move.

So here I am, in a new house, in Golden Glen, a new city far from home, and feeling incredibly sorry for myself.

I closed my eyes and waited for sleep to come. Normally on the night before my birthday, I would be happy and excited. Anticipating something fun. But this time, I was in no hurry to wake up. Sure, I thought I may get a few phone calls and messages, but without Jack or Evie with me, I knew this would be the worst birthday ever. I guess I'd just turn over, cuddle my stuffed dog Rex, and hope sleep would come fast so I wouldn't start crying again.

Chapter 2

Jack and I were in the park doing some fancy aerial acrobatics with our new drone. I had been making it dance in the air for a while and figured it was his turn. As I handed Jack the controls, he handed me the leash.

"Why don't you walk your dog around while I practice some flips and rolls," he said. So I took the leash, stroked my dog's neck, and we strolled off together. Then I saw a tennis ball on the grass. I picked it up, undid his leash, and threw it as far as I could. Which surprised me, because everybody always laughs when I try to throw a ball. But this time my arm arched back, whipped forward, and the ball soared, bounced, and rolled a long way. Like a real baseball player. And my dog ran after it as fast as he could. Then I gleefully watched him scoop it up and trot back to me. He looked like he was smiling as he dropped the ball right at my feet.

I couldn't stop smiling as I bent down to pick up the tennis ball again and again. Every time I looked down, I saw a happy dog and a ball at my feet. I threw it, and I saw my dog jump up and make an incredible catch.

I couldn't stop smiling. I was so happy as I took my arm back slowly and got ready to throw it. The sun was shining, the grass was green, and I even started to hear singing.

"Happy birthday, sleepy head! You're thirteen."

No! It was Mom crooning in a sickeningly sweet voice, waking me and shattering my dream.

How depressing. It was such a wonderful fantasy. You see, I love dogs. And every year since I was four I've asked Mom for a dog for my birthday. And every year she has some lame excuse. Two years ago when I pleaded, she told me it wasn't a good idea because animals shouldn't be confined to man-made spaces. After that ridiculous comment I decided I was finished begging. So there's no reason to wake up today. I just wanted to go back to my dream.

"Somebody's Miss Grumpy Kat this morning. I'll have you know that I made your favorite cake for dinner! With sprinkles on top!" she chirped.

"Go away," I grunted. "I'm not getting out of bed today. And let's just forget it's my birthday." I turned over and closed my eyes. Mom grabbed my hand and put something in it. It felt like a little box, but I ignored her. And as she continued to sit on my bed, I pretended to go back to sleep. Maybe if I started snoring she'd go away. I tried hard to go back to that heavenly place in my mind where I was walking my dog in the park. With my eyes closed, I started to visualize me and Jack and my dog running around the freshly cut grass. I got happy again and tightly pulled up my covers. All of a sudden I heard a sonic boom that shook my bedroom. And Mom yelled, "Bless you!"

That did it. Mark sneezed, which could trigger a massive earthquake. Now I really was awake. Once again he ruined everything. And if I were thinking clearly, I would jump out of bed and take shelter. Instead I opened one eye and looked at Mom. She wasn't leaving.

"Open your gift, honey bun," she said as she grabbed my hand that held the little box. "If you don't open it, I will," she teased. I loudly groaned but thought, *Fine, let's get this over with.* I sat up.

As I looked at the little box, I realized it's some sort of jewelry. Oh how idiotic. When do I ever wear jewelry? I rolled my eyes and figured if I opened it quickly she'd finally leave my room. So I unwrapped the paper and opened the box, and sure enough, it was a silver necklace with some type of charm hanging down. Just what I wanted.

She gave me a big kiss. "See, honey?" She announced proudly. "It's the head of a dog surrounded by turquoise stones. Knowing you love dogs, when I saw it I immediately thought of you. And this is Nevada turquoise, which has very powerful healing abilities."

I just stared at her and felt like crying. She's so clueless. But she looked so innocent and excited about that stupid gift that I didn't feel like hurting her. I decided to try to give her a little smile. And believe me, that wasn't easy.

"We have big plans today, sweetheart. Come down to breakfast and we'll tell you about them," she whispered mysteriously as she left the room.

I was miserable. I didn't want to get up. And I certainly didn't want to hear what "special plans" they had for me. But I couldn't get back to sleep. My ears were still ringing from that sneeze. I had just finished my latest Sherlock Holmes mystery. I didn't have a book upstairs to read, and I was getting hungry. So I guess I had to get up. Being unhappy, I hadn't eaten much lately, and I knew Mom would make me her fluffy matcha green tea, whole-wheat pancakes with lots of pure maple syrup. Sounds awful, but they're really good. Even if they are healthy.

I washed up, put on my slippers, and headed straight to the breakfast table. And there was Mark, hunched over his plate and chomping on his food like a wild animal. I sat down, and Mom heaped some pancakes in front of me. Mark turned and eyed them like a tiger ready to pounce. I instinctively put my hands up to protect my plate as Mom said, "Honey, we know this change has been hard for you. So Mark had an idea, and I'm going along with it. After breakfast we have one more little surprise."

"No thanks, Mom. I don't think my heart could take the excitement of another piece of jewelry." With that, Mark started laughing. Roaring actually, which hurt my ears. I didn't want to look at him in case I would see gluey mush in his mouth. So I looked down at my plate and started to spread some organic, grass-fed butter on my pancakes. I could hear him take a gulp of coffee.

"Don't worry, Kat. No more necklaces," he blurted as he put his coffee cup down with a big bang. "There's an animal shelter on my way to work. I know you love dogs, and I do too. And I think every dog deserves a home. So I talked your mother into getting you a dog."

Wh...wha...what? I froze with the knife in mid-air. As I let this information bounce around my head for a second, I looked at my knife and wanted to shout, "Well butter my butt!" But then I took a breath and realized I must have heard wrong. I still must have been dreaming. And then I heard Mom's voice.

"Yes, Kat. Mark was very convincing. I never considered the healing powers that animals, especially dogs, can have on us. I think that might be just what the doctor would order for you."

I wasn't dreaming! All I remember after that was screaming and jumping up and down. I think I ran over and hugged Mom. I may have even hugged Mark too. Then I stuffed a whole pancake into my mouth and raced off to FaceTime Evie and Jack. Yes, even with gluey mush in my mouth.

Chapter 3

We got ready, which, by the way, took Mom way too long. I just took a quick shower, brushed my teeth, and was ready to go. But Mom had to carefully select an outfit and then put on, not one necklace, but at least twenty. To say she over accessorizes is an understatement. Though that reminded me to put on my new dog necklace to show them how grateful I was about everything. I felt stupid, but it didn't look half bad.

Anyway, then Mom started in with the bracelets. She put some on one arm, and even more on the other arm. That took forever. And I haven't even gotten to her rings. Which she needed on every finger of course just to go look at dogs. Instead of watching her get ready, I had to walk around the house to keep from screaming.

Soon, another sight to behold was Mark. He came clomping downstairs looking like someone out of an old-fashioned cowboy movie. Not one that I would ever watch. He was wearing some type of work shirt tucked in, old faded jeans held up high by a thick belt and huge belt buckle, and, the icing on the cake, black pointy cowboy boots. I'd certainly never seen him wear those shoes before. And hopefully after today he'll put them back in storage. Aside from looking ridiculous on him, those boots must have been too small or something, because he was wobbling and walking funny.

After Mom put on a scarf she didn't need, she decided she was ready, and we piled into Mark's SUV. Finally, off to the shelter! As usual, Mark was singing, or I should say squawking, along with the songs on the radio. This time I politely didn't even cover my ears. But between you and me, it was torture. And for once, when he got all the lyrics wrong, I could almost handle it. Because I felt happy. A feeling I hadn't felt in a long time.

A young receptionist greeted us as we walked into the shelter and handed Mom paperwork to fill out. Really? I just wanted to see the dogs. But she said everybody has to fill out forms to enter the facility, and then she sat us at a picnic table under an umbrella to complete the task. Mom took the clipboard and pen from her. I couldn't believe how long it took her to fill out a few pages. She had to take out her glasses, read everything carefully, and slowly use her beautiful cursive penmanship. Come on, name, address, phone number...let's get going! But I tried to sit still and not complain. When I heard barking and howling in the background, though, I got really impatient. I took a few of Mom's deep yoga-type breaths she taught me to calm myself. And I must say, it worked a little. Meanwhile, Mark had taken off one of his cowboy boots and was rubbing his foot. His blue sock had a hole in it, and one long, crooked toe was exposed. Gross.

I thought I turned another year older by the time Mom finally finished those forms. Of course, she slowly got up and stretched before she handed them to the receptionist, who was now even friendlier. She quickly called out something on an intercom. Immediately, a stocky older man came out and smiled as he approached us. I'd never seen anyone who looked like him before. He had a wrinkled reddish face, long gray hair pulled back into a thin ponytail, yellow teeth, and a big white mustache that curled up towards his long nose. Suddenly I thought I was dreaming again. This couldn't be real. I was just watching a strange cartoon. I looked down, looked away, blinked a few times, and pinched myself. Ouch. Good. I'm awake, and this was really happening. As I looked back at this character, I noticed that he had a square nametag on his chest that said "Lee" in big block letters.

"Howdy," he drawled with a Southern accent as he reached to shake our hands. "How can I help y'all?"

Mom gave a big smile as she heard his thick accent, and as she opened her mouth to speak, I panicked. Oh no. She had that look in her eyes. She was going to try to be funny. And she never is. That is the one thing I can honestly say that she and Mark have in common. Thinking it cute, she might ask Lee something stupid like, "My good sir, what part of England are you from?" Okay. I only had a second. I knew I had to nip this in the bud to keep her from wasting more time, so I quickly shouted, "I want a dog."

There was a moment of silence as everyone stopped and looked at me. Was I rude? Perhaps. But Mom nodded her head and said, "That's true, Lee. We're looking for a dog to adopt. Any suggestions?"

Crisis averted. And with that, Lee cleared his throat, looked over the forms, and said, "Ya wrote here that you're open to any age or size dog." He paused. "And these pages are beautifully written, I might add."

Mom proudly smiled. Gag. "Yes," Mark piped in. "I grew up with large dogs. But..." he pointed to me. "It will be Kat's, Katherine's, decision." Mom nodded her head in agreement. Good, now we're getting somewhere.

"All right. We've got all shapes and sizes here. And some older and some young 'uns. I'll take y'all around and show you what's available."

As he opened the gate he added, "If y'all don't mind big and want a puppy, Peaches, who's very gentle, just had a litter a few months back. Her pups are ready for their forever home."

That's all I needed to hear. Of course I'd be just as happy with an older dog that needs a home, but a little puppy? Too cute.

"I'd love to look at the puppies," I tried to say respectfully. Mom started to look nervous.

"Just how big is Peaches?" she meekly asked.

Mark responded quickly, "Oh come on, it'll be fine, hon. I'd rather have a real dog. And I'm sure Kat would also." Mom looked concerned but went along with it.

Lee led us to an enclosed area where we could look in through a big glass window. I saw five of the most adorable chubby puppies I'd ever seen. They were different colors. Three were brown with various black markings, and two were black and tan. But in the corner of the room there was a very big puppy who looked out of place. He was obviously older, yellow, and had a giant black and brown speckled nose. I wondered what he was doing in with these little puppies.

"Oh, and before you ask, there's one dog in there who isn't from Peaches. He's a Labrador mix and he's a little older. He was adopted and returned to us."

That's sad, I thought. *I wonder why he was returned.* As if Lee was reading my mind, he said, "That's Kit. His last home wasn't a good fit. The family returned him because they said he was afraid of their other dog and afraid of too many other things around their house. In fact, their kids named him Scaredy Cat, but we shortened his name to Kit."

That's mean, I thought. "How long has he been here?" I asked, concerned.

"A couple months now. No one seems interested in adopting him. They say he's funny lookin'. I don't know about that, but I do have to admit that he has some issues. He's very timid and shy. Even though he's about five months old, he does better with little puppies."

As Lee was talking I noticed one of the puppies biting Kit's ear. Kit didn't respond except to let out a little cry. I couldn't stop looking at him.

"So tell us more about Peaches and these puppies," asked Mark, looking around.

"Peaches is mostly German shepherd," Lee told us. "But, ah, we never had the pleasure of meeting her mate. She had a big litter. These are the puppies we have left, and they're all males."

"You got some real active ones here. That's good. And a male dog will be fine," Mark announced. "You can really roughhouse with the big guys, and they make great watch dogs." Mom forced a smile.

I wasn't listening to Mark because I'd already fallen in love with Kit, huddled in a corner. One of the dogs ran over and jumped on him. No reaction. Then another dog came over and bit his oversized nose. He gave a little howl and once again did nothing. That's it. He needed me. And his big nose reminded me of my big ears.

"I made my decision. I want that one," I announced and pointed to Kit. Mark was watching a few other puppies wrestling with each other.

"What? Kat, that's crazy." He motioned to the brownish dog on top of the other ones. "How about him? He looks like a winner."

"No, Mark. I want that yellow one. I love him," I stated firmly. Mark started to say something but stopped himself. He shrugged. It was obvious he was disappointed.

Lee put a leash on Kit and brought him out. His nose looked even more pronounced with the glisten of doggy slobber all over it. Kit trembled as I was handed the leash.

"Yup, he's a shy one," Lee said gently. "'Bout as shaky as a leaf in a hurricane. And he may have a funny-looking nose, but it's sure a powerful one. When I pass through the play area with a treat in my pocket, even if he's sleepin', he comes a-runnin'. He can pick up that scent even when I'm way 'cross the yard. Now that's one keen sense of smell."

Mark shook his head and snickered to Mom, "He looks more like a clown to me."

"Mark, that's not nice," she answered back. She knew I could hear him, but I could tell she agreed.

"Kat, don't you want to take your time and look at the puppies some more? This is a big decision. Maybe we should have Lee bring a few out and play with them?" Mark urged desperately.

"No thanks, Mark. I'm ready to go," I answered.

Mark looked at me then threw up his hands and walked away.

Hey, I didn't care what he thought. Kit's the one for me. And I couldn't stop hugging and stroking his soft fur. And when he looked up at me with those beautiful soft brown eyes, I think he smiled. I kissed his nose and said out loud, "I love you, Kit." He licked me back.

After pacing around, Mark wandered back to us. I guess he knew that nothing he could say would change my mind, so he declared, "Okay then. Kit it is." But I could tell he was very displeased.

Lee looked at me and winked. "Oh, and you should know that pup is going to get even bigger, and he really loves to eat."

"That's okay," I told him. "So do I." Lee and I laughed. Mark did not. I looked at Mom, and she just looked dazed and confused about everything. As we headed back to the office, I took Kit for a little walk so Mom and Mark could finish up the paperwork and handle the finances. I was happy to have some alone time with my new dog. My new dog!

Kit seemed to be okay on the leash. But I noticed he wasn't eager to go far. So after tentatively exploring for a few minutes, we sat at that picnic table with the umbrella until Mom and Mark were ready to go. And Kit sat nicely. I couldn't stop staring at him and smiling. When I was petting him, I actually started giggling. I'm not a giggler, but I couldn't help myself. My dream had finally come true, and I was more excited than I'd ever been.

On the car ride home, Mom seemed a bit nervous, and Mark didn't look too happy. He was unusually quiet, which was a good thing. And I was glad he drove fast because I couldn't wait to get home and get to know Kit better. But first we had to stop at the pet store. Lucky for us, there was one on the way. Even though Lee gave us a leash and Kit already had a collar, we needed some dog food, treats, and bowls. Mark said that Kit could sleep on a cushion until we figured out what kind of bed to buy him. That seemed fine. I didn't feel like shopping. I just wanted to get home fast and start my life with my new friend.

Chapter 4

After a couple of weeks, I was pretty settled into this new house. Which meant I stayed home, flew my drone in the backyard, read my mysteries, and played with Kit every day. I pretty much kept to myself. And I never ventured outside the front door except to bring in the trash cans when asked. Mom and Mark were getting worried that I was becoming a hermit, but they heard me talking to my friends back home and figured when school started in September, I'd be forced to socialize. I was hoping that Jack would visit me soon. I told him how big and weird this house was, and he was curious to see it and the neighborhood. His dad was open to the idea, but there were some things to work out.

Kit was the sweetest dog in the world. For better or worse, Lee had described him to a tee. He had told us that Kit was very fearful. Unfortunately that's true, but I'll get to that in a minute. Lee had also told us that Kit loves food. And that he does. In a big way. Mom doesn't believe in wasting or throwing away food after dinner, so against Mark's advice, she started giving Kit table scraps.

We soon found out that Kit's favorite people foods are pork chops, stir-fry beef, baked nacho chips, cheddar cheese, any kind of chicken, and green beans. In fact, he eats all vegetables, much to the dismay of Mom and her new vegetable garden.

Now I'll get back to the fearful part. Even though Kit finally had a real home and was growing big and strong, his personality hadn't changed. He's still the scared, timid dog that we rescued from the shelter. And unfortunately I kept discovering new things that scare him. Aside from his fear of new people and other dogs, he is afraid of loud noises (he often runs from Mark), the broom, pencils, balloons, insects, and tile floors. And for some reason, he won't go in the living room. I feel sorry for him sometimes, but it makes Mark crazy. He's so insensitive. Sometimes Mark shakes his head with disgust and won't even pet him. But I love him. Kit has beautiful soft ears, kind eyes, and very fluffy yellow fur. He has that square Labrador retriever head but doesn't really have a proportionally sized nose. Actually, it takes up most of his face. So, who's perfect?

Because we were told he'd get even bigger, with Mark's suggestion, Mom had immediately enrolled Kit and me in a group training class at the park. I knew she was really hoping I would meet some neighborhood kids. But that didn't happen—there wasn't anyone close to my age. And from what I could see through my window, no one around here seems my type anyway.

Kit sure learned fast, but he clearly didn't like to be around the other dogs. When they barked, he got scared. I figured out to line up on the end so we'd only have to stand next to one dog. And thankfully, usually it was the skinny, gray hairy mutt who was also shy and spent most of the time on her back. After a few weeks of instruction, Kit knew how to sit, stay, and walk very nicely on a leash, so Mom was comfortable letting me walk him all around the neighborhood. So now, after being here three weeks, I was finally getting out of the house and taking long walks with Kit.

Mom did tell me to stay clear of the east section of the local park. That was where some homeless people were living. To be honest, when she told me not to walk near there it surprised me. Usually, Mom feels sorry for people who are down and out and would always talk to them and give them food. Even when we had very little to share. But she made me promise I'd avoid that area. She was very serious, so I did what she asked. Whatever. Maybe she knew something I didn't. Aside from my drone and books, going on long walks with Kit was the only activity that gave me any type of exercise and made me somewhat happy in this creepy new town.

Until recently, Kit was afraid to come into the kitchen because of the tiled floor. I guess he didn't like the feel of the smooth, cold tile on his paws. So he would just stand at the edge of the kitchen looking at me sadly. I solved that problem by throwing down little dishtowels on the floor so that Kit could hop from one towel to another and not have to touch the tile. Mark got so mad.

"That's ridiculous, Kat. He's a dog!" Mark barked at us. "Let him figure it out. Don't baby him like that." I ignored him.

Mom thought he'd grow out of it, but as each day passed, I didn't see any signs of Kit getting closer to outgrowing this skittish behavior. And no amount of love and affection seemed to make a difference. But I didn't care. I loved that part of him too.

Now that we'd been going on our wonderful walks, I discovered that Kit's biggest source of terror is Speedy, the yappy Chihuahua next door. Speedy belongs to a family with a teenager named Matt. I'd seen him several times, and I've heard his mother calling his name. He's much older than I am and really good looking. Evie would die. He's tall and has wavy black hair and crystal blue eyes. And girls were always hanging out in front of his house. Which wasn't great for me. A few of the girls used to try to pet Kit, but after he cringed and barked at them, they didn't go near him anymore. And now some of the girls actually make fun of his speckled nose when they think we can't hear.

Sometimes, Matt has lots of his guy friends over. They all seem to wear football jerseys. I found out he lives there with his parents and little brother Trevor, who seems to be about five years old. One day Trevor rang our bell crying. He was looking for his pet rabbit, Mr. Pickles. I guess Mr. Pickles got out and ran away. I felt bad but had to tell him that I hadn't seen the little bunny. I had a feeling that horrible Speedy had something to do with his mysterious disappearance.

Our backyards are very close and just separated by a fence. I fly my drone over the fence sometimes when I think they're not home because they have some interesting trees with branches that make good obstacle courses.

One time I guess they were home, as I overheard Matt noticing and calling Trevor to come look.

Trevor is a nice little boy. And he's cute. He always wears the same blue baseball hat and talks to us if he's on the front porch. He said he and his brother noticed my drone and told me how cool he thinks it is. Great, I'm making a friend. Too bad he's only five. Even Kit seems to tolerate Trevor. He doesn't bark at him. But as much as Kit doesn't mind Trevor, it's very hard to walk by their house when Matt is outside with Speedy. Speedy jumps up and down, barks in his high-pitched yelp, and sometimes rushes up to Kit and growls. Kit becomes terrified and freezes. I think Matt brings Speedy out of the house when he has friends over just so they can all have a good laugh.

When I complained to Mom about this, I guess she told Mark because I overheard them talking about it at the dinner table after I went upstairs. And because Mark is incapable of whispering, I could hear the whole conversation.

"What kind of dog is Kit? He's good for nothing. We can't even play a proper game of tug of war. He just lets me win." Then I heard him loudly burp. At least this time he said excuse me. "I think I'll call my old buddy Bob. He used to breed and train dogs for a living. Maybe he'll have some thoughts about how to whip that dog into shape."

Thankfully I heard Mom say, "It's not that big of a deal, Mark. He's sweet. And Kat loves him, and that's what's most important." With that I closed my door. And hugged and kissed Kit.

The next morning as we headed for the kitchen, Kit abruptly stopped and sat down. He wouldn't move. I didn't know what was wrong until I noticed a little spider on the wall in the hallway. Unfortunately Mark noticed all this too. He was behind us getting his jacket. I went and got a napkin and put the spider outside. By the way, one time Mark killed a spider, and for twenty minutes Mom gave him a long lecture about the sanctity of life of all creatures. He doesn't make that mistake anymore.

"Kat, that's the last straw. I know you love Kit, but this isn't normal behavior. I hate to say it, but he's too cowardly. I'm going to see what can be done." Mark awkwardly put on his jacket, bumped into a chair, and left, slamming the front door behind him. I was furious and held Kit tightly, hoping he didn't understand what was so rudely said.

Mark did call Bob that morning. I heard all about their conversation at dinner while I was angrily choking down my baked tofu taco. Who asked Mark to butt in anyway? And I wish he wouldn't eat and talk at the same time. Actually I just wish he wouldn't talk.

"Listen, Kat." Mark sputtered with a piece of kale between his teeth. "Bob said our dog might have a self-esteem problem. And we can deal with that. He thinks if Kit starts to feel good about himself, he'd develop more confidence and won't be as timid. He explained that dogs aren't so different from humans that way."

I just glared at him. But Mark continued anyway.

"Bob asked me if Kit is good at anything, and I remembered what that guy Lee at the shelter said about Kit's keen sense of smell. Bob thought about it and said that

Kit might excel at scent classes, hide-and-seek games, and search and rescue-type activities. And that it might be fun for both of you."

Mark was looking at me, but I looked away. There was a long silence until I decided to hear a little more. I do hate uncomfortable pauses. "Thanks for the info, but how would that help?" I asked a bit belligerently.

"Bob said if he plays these nose games and does well, he'd feel like a winner. He'd get praised and feel all sorts of positive attention. It would be good for his confidence. He'd be proud of himself."

Well, that didn't sound too bad. But I still looked down at my plate.

Mark then added, "And they use food as the reward."

Okay, now I was listening. I slowly looked up at Mark.

"I think it's a no-brainer," he said. "With Kit's love of food and good sense of smell, he recommended you try a scent class."

"I don't know. What do you do in a scent class?" I asked him after I waited a few moments on purpose.

"Bob said it's basically a game, a hunting-type game. In the beginning, the trainer hides a little piece of food in a room, and the dog uses his nose to try to find it. And when he finds it, he gets to eat it. That's the first step."

"So, I could just do that at home," I replied.

"No. There's more to it. Bob said after a while you pair the food treat with a specific odor to get the dog used to trying to find a scent. He said they use things like birch or clove oil. The dog finds that specific smell and knows his treat will be there also. Eventually you take the food away and just hide the scent, and when they find that, you hand them a treat from your pocket as a reward. And pet them. Bob explained to me that's how you build up to teaching dogs to look for certain smells, target odors."

This started to sound a little intriguing. I'd heard of drug- and bomb-sniffing dogs. Maybe that's how they start them out.

"He said the dogs have fun. It's a little complicated, I know, but I think maybe you could handle it."

Maybe I could handle it? Thank you for your confidence. But I could check this thing out. Just to show Mark, of course. Truth is, I was pretty bored, and I'd love something new to do with Kit. But I didn't say anything yet.

"Would you want to try it?" Mark asked me after a few moments.

"Sure, why not," I said casually after purposely waiting at least another minute to answer. I didn't want to give him too much pleasure. "I guess I wouldn't mind something new to do, and I do want Kit to feel good about himself. Though it probably won't work."

"Good. I'm glad you'll give it a try. And I investigated. There's a canine scent class at a doggie daycare facility not too far from here that starts on Saturday. Do you want me to enroll you?"

I nodded. But not very enthusiastically. I guess Mark does try to be helpful sometimes. But before I gave him any credit, I wanted to check out this class to see if he knew what he was talking about. Little did I know then that this suggestion, by Mark of all people, would end up changing my life.

Chapter 5

Saturday came quickly. Though I acted cool, I must admit I was excited about the scent class and got ready quickly that morning. Let's face it. I didn't have much going on these days. It turned out we were the first to arrive. Thankfully, just Mom drove us. Mark stayed home to watch sports. And she promised she'd sit in the back and be quiet. *Let's see how well that works out for me,* I thought.

After we registered and put on nametags, I sat down on a chair in a big, open room. Kit sat next to me. We positioned ourselves on the far end of the row so only one dog would be able to sit next to us. Mom told me she wanted coffee and went to the reception area. Soon, a few more people and their dogs started to arrive. And of course, Kit started getting nervous. "You'll like this," I reassured him. "You get to find food and eat it." That seemed to calm him down a little.

There were five dogs total in the class, all on leashes. There was a basset hound led in by a short, heavyset guy who was all smiles. That is, until he sat down and his dog slobbered all over his pants. I tried not to laugh. Next, a German shepherd waltzed in cautiously with his owner. He was an older man with a pointed nose and was wearing an open shirt and lots of jewelry. *Hey, maybe he'd like to borrow my necklace some time,* I thought.

Soon a beagle came prancing in with a skinny girl who looked to be in her twenties. She was nervously gesturing and talking loudly on her phone. Her beagle barked a few times, startling Kit. Thankfully, they didn't sit next to us. And finally a beautiful golden retriever arrived wagging his tail. He was with a tall young man who looked friendly and had the same color hair as his dog. I'm happy they sat next to me. The dog seemed sweet and went to sniff Kit, but Kit almost jumped onto my lap. I stroked him to calm him down. Mom came back in with a cup of coffee. She took a seat across the room in the back. She looked around and waved at me but seemed a little disappointed. I knew what she was thinking. It was obvious I was the youngest person there, and she was hoping I'd make some friends.

The trainer walked in and introduced herself. "Hello, everybody. I'm Jody. This is our beginning four-week scent class, and I hope you all enjoy. As a little background if you don't know, a dog's sense of smell, depending on the breed, is at least a thousand times more sensitive than ours. For example we may smell vegetable soup, but a dog smells each individual ingredient." We all chuckled.

"Practically speaking, this means that dogs can be trained to remember scents and locate them, even if the scent is hidden or far away."

Interesting, I didn't know that. Unfortunately, now the beagle was howling, driving Kit and me a little crazy. Jody didn't seem too happy about it either but kept talking.

"That ability makes dogs excellent partners for our military, the police, and really anyone else doing search and rescue work. In this class, we'll play search games, and you'll see how dogs are trained to do this type of work."

We were over it, but the skinny girl was still giggling about the soup joke. "Every single vegetable?" she asked. Jody stopped and patiently smiled.

"Yes. Dogs' noses are so powerful they can detect one tablespoon of sugar in the amount of water it would take to fill two Olympic-sized swimming pools. But let's move on."

Wow, I was impressed. I looked over at Mom, and she smiled and gave me a big wave again. Like we hadn't seen each other for three years. I hoped nobody saw that. In fact, I wished she'd go get another cup of coffee.

Kit was being very good, just sitting by my side at this point. And finally, the beagle was quiet. Jody talked about dogs a little more, then she picked up ten cardboard boxes and placed them in the center of the room in no particular order. After that was done, she reached into a bag, pulled out something, held it up for us to see, and then put it in one of the boxes.

"Find the hot dog," she announced. "That's the game for now. And don't be discouraged. The first time your dog tries this, he or she may not know what's going on. But eventually, they'll smell the hot dog and want to eat it." I smiled because this sounded like it could be Kit's dream game. Jody continued. "So that's it for now. Find the hot dog. And pet and praise your dog when they do. You'll notice by their third or fourth try they'll catch on to what we're doing and rush to find the treat."

Yes, this had real potential and might be easy for Kit. As I gave him a scratch behind his ear, he licked his lips. I think he smelled that little hot dog from here. Without thinking I glanced over at Mom, and again she smiled and waved. I quickly looked away. So embarrassing.

Jody walked around the room, sizing up the dogs. "Now this is important," she stated. "Notice that even if I move the boxes around, I place the treat in the same box each time, wherever it is. It has a tiny black ink mark on top. I do this so only one box has the hot dog smell. I don't want to contaminate all the boxes with the scent. After a few turns, I will move the boxes around the room and even add more boxes. That's how eventually I'll make the game more challenging. But today we'll keep it pretty simple. Now, if you practice this at home, and I hope you all do, you can use any of your dog's favorite treats. But today it's hot dogs. Everybody okay with that?"

We all nodded our heads yes. I think I nodded a little more vigorously than anybody else.

"If there are no questions, let's get started." She looked around for a moment, but we were all quiet. Well, almost all of us. The skinny girl's cell phone went off, and her little beagle was making noise again. As Jody glared at her, she reached into her purse and silenced it.

"Okay, when it's your turn, I want you to come to the center of the room and ask your dog to sit. Then please say their name, get their attention, and give them the command, which is 'search.' For example, when I do this with my dog, first I have her sit and look at me. It's important to get their attention. Then I say firmly, 'Angel, *search.*' And off we go."

Kit should be good at this. I just hoped we wouldn't have to go first.

"Who wants to go first?" Jody asked and looked at me.

Thankfully one hand was quickly raised. It was the skinny girl with the beagle. "Okay, Samantha, come up here with Savannah," Jody said and motioned for them to come up.

Samantha took her dog, Savannah, to the center of the room and asked her to sit. Oh boy. Samantha, Savannah. Tomato, tommahto, potato, pottahto. How ridiculous. Evie would be laughing with me. Anyway, Savannah sat, and Samantha said in a screechy voice, "Search!" Savannah turned and started pulling to go outside, but she was led back to the boxes. They started walking around them. Savannah looked confused, but I guess she must have caught the hot dog scent, because she went over to one box to investigate. She poked her nose at the box, trying to get it open, and Jody leaped up. "That's it, good girl. You found it! Open it up and give Samantha, I mean Savannah, the hot dog."

Savannah happily ate the piece of meat while Samantha and Jody praised her. That was their turn—they sat down. Jody then looked around to see who wanted to go next. Again she looked at me, but I looked away. Out of the corner of my eye I saw her motion to the shepherd and his owner.

"Tony, let's see how your dog does," she said with a smile. Tony stood up with his black T-shirt and gold chains around his neck. He and his black and gold shepherd trotted to the middle of the room. Tony had his dog sit and then said, "Search, Klaus!" He gave a little tug on the leash, and they started walking around the boxes. Klaus looked a little confused as they weaved in and out of the boxes. After about four minutes, with Tony getting frustrated, Jody came over to the box with the hot dog.

"Here, Klaus," she said as she flipped the box open and grabbed the treat. Klaus came over, and she fed it to him. He didn't seem that interested.

"Don't worry about it, Tony. He'll catch on to the game next time," she told him as they sat down.

"Klaus isn't really food oriented. He doesn't get that excited about meals," Tony said to Jody as they sat down.

"Okay. In that case, does he have a favorite toy?" Tony nodded yes. "Then when you practice this game at home, use that toy as his reward." Tony thought about it, nodded again, and sat down.

Then Jody told us to distract our dogs so they wouldn't watch her as she again hid another piece of hot dog. This time she walked right over to me, looked at my nametag, and said, "Your turn, Katherine."

"You can call me Kat," I told her softly as I nervously stood up. Kit followed me to the middle of the room, and I told him to sit. I then looked at Kit's face, petted him, and said, "Kit, *search*." I gave his leash a little pull, and we started walking around the boxes. Kit took one sniff in the air and headed straight for the box with the hot dog. *This is going to be easy*, I thought. Wrong. Suddenly that stupid beagle barked and made a growling sound.

Kit stopped and sat down before he got to the box. He froze and wouldn't go one step further.

"You can do this, Kit," I whispered to him, gently pulling on his leash. "You love hot dogs." But Kit was too scared to go to the box because he would have to pass by that obnoxious beagle.

After a few uncomfortable moments, Jody came over, took the treat out of the box, and gave it to Kit, who gobbled it up. "It's all right, Kat," she said warmly to me. "He'll get it next time." We went back to our seat.

I must admit, I felt defeated and very sad for Kit. I don't know why, but I did look up at Mom again, who just smiled and waved. That wasn't helpful. I started to think that Kit may never be able to overcome his fears. So I started to pet him and said into his ear, "Don't worry, Kit. Whatever happens, I still love you." But truthfully, I got a little sad.

Next, the basset hound, Charlie, took a turn and found the treat pretty quickly. And the golden retriever, Wally, who went last, walked around for a few minutes with his owner, Glenn, then rolled over and wanted to be tickled. After a while Jody gave him the treat, and they sat down while Jody announced that it was time for the second round.

Samantha got up and took Savannah to the center of the room. Savannah looked back at Kit, and he cowered next to me. Samantha then said, "Savannah, *search*," unfortunately, once again, in an unpleasant tone. Maybe she was Mark's long lost daughter. Anyway, Savannah then took off, quickly walking in between the boxes until she suddenly stopped and peed. Jody popped up.

"No, no, no," Jody scolded. Savannah didn't care and finished her business. Samantha just stood there. "Somebody please grab me those paper towels and that spray bottle," Jody called as she quickly approached the mess. Glenn, who was closest, jumped up to help. Samantha did nothing. Jody took Savannah's leash and pulled her away from the area.

"Samantha, please take your dog for a short walk to make sure she's finished relieving herself." Samantha took her dog, and they left the room in a hurry.

"Some dogs do this to mark their territory," Jody said to us. "And it's not acceptable. They forfeit their turn when they do this," Jody continued as she and Glenn wiped everything up. After they were finished, Jody looked at me and said, "Kat, without Savannah here, it may be a good time for you to take your turn."

She was right. With that pest gone, I thought we had a chance. I took a deep breath and stood up. We went to the center of the room, and Kit sat obediently. I looked at him and said firmly, "Kit, *search.*"

To my surprise, Kit took one sniff and headed straight for the box with the treat. He knocked over the box, and Jody called out, "Good job, Kit."

He happily ate his pieces of hot dog. I hugged him and shouted, "Good, Kit! Good boy!" I did not look over at Mom. I almost did, but I stopped myself. Jody rushed over to us and gave Kit a big pat on the back. We skipped back to our seats.

Each of us had eight turns. Jody kept adding more boxes. On Kit's third turn, Savannah barked a little, but Kit was able to ignore her and concentrate on finding the treat. I had given him a light breakfast that morning, and I guess he wasn't about to let the other dogs get all the hot dogs. On the fourth try, Jody paired a scent, a target odor, with the treat. She used a Q-tip dipped in clove oil placed in a little glass jar. I found out it was a baby food jar that had been cleaned and had a few holes punched in the lid. She put the hot dog and the little jar with the Q-tip together in the same box. Every time the dog would find the hot dog, there would also be that clove scent. Unfortunately, by this time, the nice guy with the golden retriever had left. Wally just wasn't interested in the game. And finally, I'm happy to report, Savannah had calmed down. She did quite well, actually.

By the end of our session, Jody told us that during the next class she was going to take away the hot dog, and we were going to ask our dogs just to find the clove scent and that they would get their treat when they do. "I'm changing the game a bit." She grinned. "This is the next step in doing nose work."

She then explained that we are to reward our dog with food the moment they find the scent. She advised us to wear clothing with pockets so that we could hide the treats in them. When our dog found the target scent, the Q-tip dipped in clove oil, we should immediately reward them with a treat from our pocket. "Again, you should reward them as soon as they discover the scent. Be swift about it," she emphasized. "And always lavish them with praise."

She then gave us all a baby food jar, Q-tips, and a little container of oil. "This is so you can practice the game at home. And for now, make sure you practice indoors."

With that, she said goodbye, and we all got up to leave. I met Mom outside, who was on her third cup of coffee. Great. She'll be hyper and babble non-stop on the ride home. And she did. But I didn't mind. I was thinking about my day and how well it went. And I couldn't wait to practice this at home.

I read my mystery novels, took walks, and played the search game with Kit most of the week. I did meet a few adults on my walks, and we smiled at each other. Sometimes they went to pet Kit, but he would shrink, so they would just walk on. When I would pass girls who looked closer to my age, they never said hello.

I tried to explain to Evie about the scent class. She likes dogs, but I don't think she got it. Mark understood. And after I told him about the class, he brought home more boxes from work for me to use. That was nice of him. Kit and I did practice every day, but Jody had said not to do it for more than fifteen minutes at a time. Apparently, it's very tiring for the dog.

The next Saturday finally came, and I think Kit could tell we were going to do something special. He had a little extra skip to his step. I ate a quick breakfast, Mark wished us good luck, and Mom drove us to class. On the way there, she told me that if I didn't mind, she'd drop me off and then come back and pick me up. I wanted to shout whoopee. Instead I just casually said okay.

The following week, there were only four dogs. As expected, golden boy and his lovely golden retriever had dropped out. And this time, Jody brought a huge bag of cut up cheese. I knew Kit would be very happy with this choice.

For our first round, Jody put out the boxes and still paired the scent with a piece of cheese. But on our second try, she took the cheese away, and the dogs were just searching for the clove scent. It took another few turns for most of the dogs to realize now what was expected of them, but Kit caught on quickly. He figured out that I would hand him a piece of cheese if he located the box with the clove scent. The irritating Savannah also caught on pretty quickly. The German shepherd wasn't doing as well but finally got it at the end of class. It was cute. Every time Klaus found the correct box, Tony would give him a little stuffed animal. And he squeaked it as they took their seats.

When it was Kit or Savannah's turn, Jody started really making it complicated. She added lots more boxes and moved them around the room. But that didn't confuse Kit. It only took him a few seconds to find the target odor. He was the best in the class. He certainly enjoyed the praise, and even more, the pieces of cheese. And in some way, I think he enjoyed competing. Mom came back just as we were finishing our last turn, and she looked very impressed.

As we were leaving, Jody remarked, "Your dog might have a real future in this. He was very impressive today." I just smiled back, but I could feel my face burning. I was so proud. Thankfully Mom must not have had as much coffee because she didn't start rambling. She just said thank you to Jody, and we got in the car.

We took nose classes all summer long. In fact after we finished the second level, Jody asked me if I wanted some private sessions. I had to ask Mom and Mark, as I knew this would be more expensive. Mom looked like she was thinking about it, but to my surprise, Mark said sure, whatever I wanted. So I invited Mark to come along, and even he was impressed with Kit's talent. After completing the next level, which was more complex, Kit could find the target odor even when Jody tried to fool him with the scent in a really far corner, or high on a table, covered with a blanket. He even found the scent when she hid it in another room. He loved this game, and it brought us even closer. Because we were now getting private lessons twice a week, Kit and I were up to the third level of nose work. It was getting to be very advanced stuff.

Unfortunately, Jack hadn't been able to come visit me, but he promised he'd try over spring break. But truthfully, I had been keeping busy and wasn't as lonely as I had been. I did tell Mom and Mark over dinner one night how much I missed laughing with Evie. Mark knew her family doesn't have much money and said that maybe for my next birthday, he'd pay for Evie to come out here. That would be a great birthday present, even if it's a year away. I decided that her visit would be more pleasurable than another necklace from Mom. So yes, I missed home, but I guess I was doing okay. However, summer was ending, and it was time for me to start school. And I was getting nervous about that.

Chapter 6

As expected, I didn't sleep for more than one hour the night before my first day of school. I felt like a robot as I showered and brushed my teeth. And I was trying to make my hair behave, but it was curling in really funny ways. They say high humidity does that and, let me tell you, it's true. It didn't look good. In fact, my hair seemed to shrink up overnight and curl around my ears, which was making them look particularly big today.

After that, it took me way too long to get dressed. I had planned what to wear the night before, but for some reason that outfit didn't work. Maybe it was because of my big hair, puffy eyes, and ears sticking out. I don't know. So I just put on a black T-shirt and my best pair of black jeans. All black. Because that was just about how cheerful I felt. But as I looked in the mirror, something happened. I started to feel angry that I cared this much about how I looked. So I decided to do something bold. I usually just wear little studs in my ears not to call attention to their size. But for my first day of school, that wasn't what I was going to do. I found these huge, colorful hoop earrings that Mom made years ago, which I had never worn for obvious reasons. I felt so mad at this situation that I decided to show that I didn't care what anybody thought. I am who I am. So I slipped on the earrings, tucked my hair behind my ears, stood up straight, and felt a little better about myself. I did take a couple of selfies and sent them to Jack and Evie. I knew they'd crack up.

I didn't eat anything for breakfast. I just wasn't hungry. If anything, I was feeling sick to my stomach. Mom made me a peanut butter and jelly sandwich for lunch— she called it comfort food. But I was sure I wouldn't be hungry then either. I knew she felt bad for me and was just pretending everything was normal. She drove me to school and thankfully knew not to try to give me a pep talk. Which was wise. I would have snapped her head off. As I got out of the car, I felt all foggy walking into school. Like I was in a dream. Or nightmare, I should say. But I tried to hold my hold my head up high as I walked into my first class. I sat down, took a deep breath, and watched as everyone arrived.

A frilly-looking girl who took a seat on the side of the room was one of the girls I'd seen on my walks with Kit. She didn't even look at me. I quickly looked away. As more kids filed in, it was obvious they all knew each other. And that no one was wearing my brand of jeans or sandals. So I busied myself pretending to be organizing my backpack. Then I heard a girl's voice say, "Hi, I'm Ella." I looked up and realized she was talking to me. I weakly smiled and introduced myself in a shaky voice. She smiled back and sat next to me. I was thinking of something to say to her when two other girls rushed in and sat next to her. They were happy to see each other, and, once again, I was invisible. I think one of the girls, her name was Brianna, gave me a dirty look when I asked Ella a question. Okay. She's pretty scary.

Our teacher arrived and introduced herself. She announced that we have a peanut allergy in our classroom so we couldn't bring any peanut products to school. Yep, peanut butter is made from peanuts, so there went my comfort food. I tossed it into the nearest trash bin. I suppose I could start to use our jar of peanut butter at home as the target scent for Kit. If I can't eat it, somebody should. Peanut butter is another food on Kit's list of favorites. As I was throwing my lunch away, I did think to save the apple in case I happened to get an appetite later.

I felt like I was in a trance as we were all introduced. I remember the teacher talking, writing down assignments, and going to a couple other classrooms. Everything felt weird. It was all so different than back home. And then it was lunchtime. I was glad I saved that apple, as taking a few bites at least gave me something to do. But I was far from hungry. Everyone seemed to have friends to sit with, so I wandered around and sat alone outside. Then the bell rang, I had a few more classes, there was Mom's car, and I got in. It was all a blur. I do clearly remember seeing Kit in the back seat though, climbing in and hugging him. Again, wise of Mom not to ask me how my day went.

Chapter 7

The first week went by slowly, and sorry to say, nothing got any better. Except I became more familiar with the routine, so I stopped feeling quite as lost. Right away, I found out that Brianna is the mean girl in the grade. There's always one of them. Apparently, she's really rich and stuck up about it. Her dad owns some of the stores in town, like the hardware store and the dry cleaners, and her grandfather used to be the mayor. I better stay away from her. I'm not sure, but I thought I heard her making fun of my ears the other day. And a couple of her friends seemed to be laughing along. At least Ella wasn't one of them, but because she's in that group, I guess she's not a potential friend. Hey, I'm not surprised. I didn't expect to make any.

The homework was easy enough, which gave me plenty of time to play with Kit when I got home. Boy, he's getting good at search games. Just the other day I put some peanut butter on the Q-tip, placed it in the glass baby jar with the holes poked it in, put it in a baggie, zipped it in my backpack, and hid it in the top of my closet. No problem for Kit. And he's starting to like hide-and-seek. That's a new game we're playing—he could find me anywhere. Aside from that, Jack and I have been FaceTiming a lot lately, as he's building a new drone and needs my help. This one will have a bigger motor so we'll get a longer flight time. And it will go faster and have a better quality camera. All very exciting. I can't wait until he visits. So at least I've had things to do and something to look forward to.

Sometimes Mom asks me questions about school, but I don't want to get into it with her. She knows I'm unhappy. But to be a little positive, which I know is important to her, and because I'm still grateful about Kit, I did tell her that I like my science teacher. I actually really do. She's a dog lover and very interesting. We talked one day after class. That's about all I told Mom about school. The truth is, it's hard to tell Mom what I'm really thinking. She usually doesn't listen. Or she interrupts with her own thoughts about something completely unrelated. For example, a few days ago she asked me once again about school, and I started to tell her about a guy in history class I'd seen on my walks. And that he asked me why I would want such a wimpy dog with a funny nose. Mom was quiet for a moment and then said, "Oh, did I tell you? I think I'm going to have a stall at the craft fair to display my artifacts and jewelry. Nothing fancy, but it will be something to get me started. What were you saying, sweetheart?"

So forget it, I thought, and I continued to tell her very little. I guess I really don't mind that she's so spacey. I didn't feel like talking to her or Mark about school

47

anyway. I was still so mad at them for making me move here. But there's nothing I could do about it for now, so what's the point.

Surprising me though, just when I thought my mom didn't understand what was going on with me, she said the other day, "Kat, give things some time. I know it must be difficult for you. I'm sorry. Girls are tough at your age, and it takes time to make friends. So I was thinking. I know you love reading, and books make good company. For a while, why don't you take a book to school and read in the library during lunch."

I thought about what she said. I don't know. It's a little pathetic, but it might be better than sitting alone. It certainly wouldn't help me make any friends, but at least it will give me something to do. Thinking that I'll most likely get anointed Queen Nerd, I called June back home, who people always used to call nerdy.

"Just look confident and pretend you don't care," she advised. "What do you care what people think? When you get out of that place and you're successful, you can laugh at how stupid they are the rest of your life."

It turned out that reading a book during some breaks and at lunchtime was a nice way to pass the time. Now I'm reading a book about using hide-and-seek as a game for search and rescue training. It's very interesting. And this quiet break in my day puts me in a better mood to get through it.

Jody, the scent class trainer, kept in touch with me. Apparently, she really thought Kit could be a star in this field. She knew I was back in school but asked me if I wanted to continue my training privately on the week-ends. Private lessons are costly, and Mom wasn't crazy about the idea, but Mark said—I mean blared—that it was okay. I was grateful about that. So now I had something to do on Saturdays. Which was great, because Brianna and her friends were talking about soccer tryouts the upcoming Saturday. How sad, now I wasn't available. By the way, I'm about as good at soccer as Mark is at whispering.

Chapter 8

The following week, to my horror, Mark's boss at work informed him how good our middle school soccer team has been over the years. And that apparently, they were in first place last year. Like I care. Mark happily shared how nice he thought it was that his boss was taking an interest in helping us fit in. I smiled but thought it would be nicer if he'd just butt out. It was because of his big mouth that over dinner, Mark lectured me about the value of playing a school sport. And how wonderful soccer is. And how great he was in high school. Help me. I could just picture Mark stumbling and tripping down the field and then kicking the ball into the goal by accident.

Anyway, no worries. Thankfully, the team had already been chosen. But did that fact calm Mark down? Hardly. During dessert he felt the need to regale Mom and me with his soccer skills and the time he singlehandedly won a tournament for his team by scoring the final goal. I just rolled my eyes. Even Mom didn't seem impressed. I guess she'd heard that story a hundred times before. Mark also eagerly suggested that he could teach me some of his fancy footwork if I was interested. Well, I'm not. Period. End of story...I thought.

I was horrified to discover it wasn't the end of the story. Mark asked me if I'd do him a favor and go with him to the park some Saturday and watch our soccer team play. He said we'd have fun. Fun? I wanted to shout that I'd rather have my fingernails pulled out, but what could I do? He had just written a check to pay Jody for another four weeks of private sessions. Really now, how rude could I be? Yep. Not rude enough, because guess where we ended up the following Saturday. Just my luck, Jody had called on Wednesday night telling me that she was sick and couldn't have our class that Saturday. And Mark overheard.

"Hey, Kat. That means, on Saturday, you've got nothing going on. Here's our chance. How 'bout we go to the park and watch the girls' soccer team's first game?" He was almost frothing with excitement. I thought for a moment and realized I was dead in the water.

"Sure, Mark. We can go," I answered him flatly. Then I thought fast. "But only if I can bring Kit along. He's very disappointed that our class was cancelled." At least I'd have a distraction and wouldn't have to talk to Mark the whole time.

He looked overjoyed and started nodding his head, making it almost fall off. "If it makes you happy, bring Kit." So that's how we ended up at the park early Saturday morning.

Chapter 9

I woke up gloomy that Saturday thinking about spending the day at the park with Mark. Watching a game I have no interest in whatsoever. Oh well. Sometimes you just have to bite the bullet. Mark was hyper and bouncing around the house that morning. I was moving very slowly. After breakfast, we took off. He did think to bring water and a couple of fold-up chairs, which was a good idea. They were quite comfortable, and Kit was happy lying underneath mine. After a while, I put Kit's leash on the ground. I didn't need to hold it. He was huddling near me and wasn't going anywhere.

When we first arrived on the field, the atmosphere was tolerable. Probably because no one was there yet. But after about fifteen minutes, people started drifting in, and then I saw Brianna arrive with her mother. Yikes. That reminded me how much I didn't want to be there. Of course, she gave me a scary dirty look. I think her mother did too. She was wearing a fancy sweater and tons of gold jewelry. I'm not a fashion expert, but that look didn't seem appropriate for a Saturday morning kids' soccer game.

Shortly after that, a few of Brianna's friends arrived, and the girls started practicing. Just watching them practice was beyond boring. I looked at Mark, assuming he would feel the same way, but he looked deliriously happy. At least I was glad that Kit didn't seem nervous. He was comfortable hiding under the chair, being close to me.

Then I saw Ella arrive at the park with a group of boys. When she's not around her crowd, she's pretty nice. She does say hi to me, and we've talked a little. Those rowdy guys must be her brothers, because they resembled her, were also all in soccer uniforms, and were all running toward the field. And a frazzled woman, probably her mom, was following them slowly with an ice chest.

Mark saw me watching them and smiled nostalgically. "She must be the snack mom today." I looked at him quizzically, so he explained that every week, a different family is in charge of bringing refreshments for the team. And he told me what his mother would bring when she was snack mom. Something about water, oranges, and cookies, but I stopped listening. It did look like Ella's family brought cookies, because there were a bunch of pink cardboard cookie boxes, and now they were all arguing over whose boxes were whose. I guess all her brothers had games today too. When her mother approached, she tried to help sort things out, but Ella seemed aggravated because she was late and just quickly grabbed a couple of boxes. She then put them on the table set up near the coach, and ran out onto the field.

We watched the game in silence for quite some time. I was daydreaming until... "Hi," I heard someone say softly.

I thought that little voice was directed at me, so I slowly turned around. And there was Trevor, my next-door neighbor smiling at me. "Hi, Trevor," I answered back.

"Can I pet your dog? It's Kit, right?" he asked sweetly.

"Yes it is, Trevor. But remember, he's very shy," I warned him. Wisely I got on the ground with Trevor, and we both stroked Kit's back. To my surprise, Kit was very happy with the attention from him. After a minute or so, his older brother Matt walked up to us. All the girls on the field stopped and looked over at him. Really. That's how cute he is. But when he approached, Kit got nervous and barked.

"Come on, Trevor," Matt said, ignoring Kit and briefly glancing at me.

"It's Kit," Trevor said happily. "And she's the girl with the drone."

"Yeah, I know. Hi," he added, a little more friendly.

Mark looked at them with a big clown smile. "Hello, boys!"

"Hey," answered Matt, turning to him briefly. Trevor just looked up at him curiously. I guess he'd never seen such a goofy man.

Matt turned his attention back to me, "What kind of drone do you have?" he asked.

"A brushless quadcopter," I answered. "My friend and I built it ourselves. It's good for racing and agility."

"Very cool," Matt responded. There was a moment of silence.

"Hey I'm sorry if I've flown it over your backyard a couple of times. I was using your trees for practice. Don't worry. I wasn't recording anything."

Matt laughed. "No problem. There isn't much to see out back. Except Speedy chasing squirrels."

Trevor continued to pet Kit, and I rose to sit back in my seat.

"You can fly it sometime if you want," I said casually.

Matt's face brightened. "Thanks. That would be cool."

Trevor looked up at me and asked, "Me too?"

"Sure. I could teach you." Trevor continued petting Kit. Matt started watching the game.

Suddenly Mark's cell phone went off. As he fumbled around for it in his pocket he blurted, "Kat, excuse me." He then looked to see who was calling. "I need to take this." He jumped up and looked frantic. "I think we have some problems at work."

With that he turned, answered his phone awkwardly, banged his knee, and walked away from us.

A whistle blew, and I guessed it was halftime. Ella's mom started pouring water or something into cups and putting out sliced oranges. She also put out napkins and arranged the cookie boxes. Everyone went over to the table and was getting something to drink and an orange.

Trevor got up. "I hear you playing some kind of game with Kit. Is it hide-and-seek?" Kit now got up, stretched, and sat beside me.

"We do that too," I answered. "And we also play a nose game. I hide a scent, a specific smell, and Kit has to find it. He's very good at it. He can find things anywhere."

"What kind of scent?" asked Trevor innocently. I could tell that Matt was also listening.

"Lately, I've been using peanut butter. I put some peanut butter on a little piece of cotton and hide it. And he finds it wherever it is. We take classes. He's becoming a trained scent dog," I answered patiently. Thankfully Mark was still off somewhere blabbing.

"Oh. I like peanut butter too. How does he know when the game starts?" Kit licked Trevor's hand.

"The game starts when I say, 'Kit, search!'"

With that, Kit looked at me and took off towards the picnic table set up with all the snacks. I stared in horror as he jumped up and put his paws onto the flimsy table. It almost collapsed. He then barked at one of the cookie boxes. All the soccer girls and their moms came running. Matt, Trevor, and I dashed over there.

"No, Kit!" I called out and reach for his leash. But he continued to bark and nosed a box until it fell to the ground. All the cookies spilled out of it.

Ella's mom shrieked, and Brianna's mother viciously shouted, "Get that dirty dog away from there!"

"Great!" Brianna said. "Now some cookies are on the grass!"

I picked up the leash and pulled Kit away from the table. Brianna's mom started picking the cookies up.

"Hey, wait a second. What kind of cookies are these?" she asked in surprise as she picked up two cookies and examined them.

"I brought chocolate chip and oatmeal raisin for the girls," answered Ella's mom.

Brianna's mom said in a shocked voice, "No. Look! These have nuts on them!"

"They can't. I told them no nuts," Ella responded defensively.

"Well these two have peanuts on top," Brianna's mom said angrily. "I know what peanuts look like!"

"Can't be. I know about Brianna's allergy. I would never bring anything with nuts to our game," Ella's mom said as she reached for the cookies.

She looked at them in horror.

"You're right. I don't know how this happened," she said, clasping her hand over her mouth in horror.

Ella grabbed her mom's arm. "Sorry, Mom. Maybe I grabbed the wrong box. When Dylan picked them up from the bakery he told them he wanted some fancy chocolate chip cookies for his team. With sprinkles, M&M's, and nuts. He thought it was okay if we were careful they didn't touch any of the others. And he was careful to label the box."

There was a complete silence. She continued.

"I'm sorry. I guess they got mixed up. Sorry, Brianna."

Brianna didn't look at her.

Brianna's mother listened then shook her head and was still furious. "Do you know what would have happened if Brianna ate one of these cookies?"

Ella's mother meekly nodded. "Yes. We're so sorry. It was a terrible mistake. I should never have let the children take care of this. Please forgive me." She picked up the box on the ground and saw a big black X marked on the side. "Yes, that is what must have happened. It was an accident. And we are so very sorry. This will never happen again."

There was a moment of silence as Brianna's mom continued to fume. Ella's mother then added, "How about I take everybody out for ice cream after the game?"

All the girls looked at each other, smiled, and happily nodded. Everyone seemed okay about the incident except Brianna and her mother.

"I guess that dog saved the day," announced Ella gratefully.

Brianna's mom scoffed. "I suppose we were lucky that dumb dog jumped up to eat the cookies. But he looks diseased. Get him out of here." Brianna's mother turned and gestured to me. Suddenly Matt walked right up to her.

"Hey, lady, he's not a dumb dog. He knew what he was doing. He was looking for peanuts and found them."

"What are you talking about?" she snapped back at him. "He's a wild dog and wanted cookies and luckily knocked those over." But Matt didn't back down.

"Wrong. He has had professional scent training. He was following a scent," Matt announced. "Kat has been training this dog, and peanut butter is one of the scents she has him find. He was doing his job."

"Good boy, Kit!" Trevor added.

Everyone got quiet. I knew I had to say something.

"Yes, Kit takes nose work classes, and he has been searching for peanut butter lately. He thought I asked him to find it," I said.

Brianna's mom just shook her head with disbelief. Everybody else was listening but looked confused. Just then, the whistle blew.

"Whatever," she muttered as the girls ran back onto the field.

"All I know is a dog like this shouldn't be by food. We don't want any parasites. So take him away. Far away."

I turned, and we slunk back to our chairs. Matt and Trevor followed.

"Thanks, Matt," I said to him.

"No problem. She was out of line," he said angrily as he took Trevor's hand. They turned to leave. "Your dog was just doing his job. And it was very impressive. I don't like that family." He then said, "We gotta go, see ya around." Trevor waved at me, and they left.

Just then Mark came bouncing back to us and folded up his chair.

"I'm so sorry, Kat, but we can't stay. I gotta drop you off at home and go into work. Major issues. I hope you're not too disappointed."

Disappointed? Well, that was not exactly how I'd describe my feelings after hearing this information. Try elated. I quickly folded my chair up, pulled Kit, and almost ran to the car.

Mark was distracted on the drive home and didn't even turn the radio on. At one point he did ask what that "hubbub" (his word) was around the picnic table during halftime. I said it was nothing. I wasn't in the mood to discuss it with him. I wasn't sure how he'd react. So, for once we drove in silence, and he dropped me off at home.

Even though today was a bit of a disaster, I was very proud of Kit. I knew he was a hero, even if those stupid soccer people didn't think so. And I couldn't believe Matt defended us. Of course, he's much older than me, and we can't really be friends, but he's a great guy. And Trevor is a sweet kid. I like them. And it didn't hurt my standing in school that all the girls witnessed Matt sticking up for me.

Chapter 10

Mom was meditating with the door closed when Kit and I came home. She wasn't expecting us to be home so soon. Quite honestly, neither was I, and I was thrilled to have a quiet house. Sometimes, Mom does her yoga and meditates for hours. So I grabbed something to eat, went up to my room, and relaxed. By the time I went downstairs in the late afternoon, Mark had come home, and he and Mom were heatedly discussing something. Mom didn't ask how my day at the park was; she was distracted, and I decided not to bring it up. Partially because I hoped the subject of soccer would never ever be brought up again.

The rest of the weekend was uneventful. Mark had to spend a lot of time at his office. Nothing wrong with that! Evie called on Sunday, which was nice, and invited me to come stay with her over Christmas. Initially, I was over the moon excited, but then I thought about leaving Kit. Even though it would just be for four days, and even though I was dying to spend some time with her, I had to think about this one. I told her I'd ask Mark and Mom and tell her next week. I wish she could come here. Hopefully next year.

Interestingly, school on Monday was a little different. Still, of course, no one really talked to me, but I felt like some of the girls were whispering when I passed and looking at me differently. Some even smiled at me. Except for Brianna. She gave me even more ugly, evil, mean looks all day. I knew people were talking about Kit and the peanut butter ordeal because my science teacher asked me if I could come to her office during lunch. She wanted to hear what really happened at the park. Boy, these things travel. I told her about Kit and what he did, and she wanted to know what's involved in nose work. Being a fellow dog lover, she was interested in hearing details and all about the training involved. We talked almost like friends. And I found out that she's interested in drones too. She even asked me questions about where I used to live and why we moved here. She said it was obvious that I wasn't happy and she hoped things would get easier soon.

I found myself opening up and telling her all about home and Evie and Jack and how we built our drones. And how much I love crime novels and mysteries. I couldn't stop talking. She asked me how I felt about the mystery surrounding our house. What? Mystery about my house? I told her I didn't know what she was talking about. She was surprised that I hadn't heard anything about the scandal. Scandal? Wow. What was Mom keeping from me? I told Ms. Getty that all my parents ever said was that Mark's company got our big beautiful house at a really good price. I begged her to fill me in, but she told me to ask my parents about it first. She wasn't comfortable gossiping. And just then, the bell rang. I had to get back to class.

When I got home, I asked Mom and Mark if they knew anything about the history of our house. About some mystery or scandal that might have happened here. They were suddenly quiet. They just looked at each other and shook their heads no. And then looked down. Hmmm. Their body language screamed that they did know something but didn't want to tell me. That's interesting. I didn't feel like pushing it with them. The truth would be all sugarcoated anyway. I'll try to get the real scoop from Ms. Getty or somebody else at school.

For some reason, the next couple of days passed pretty quickly. It was already Thursday, and I was looking forward to seeing Jody on Saturday. I tabled the house topic for now, as I wasn't sure who to approach. But I have been talking to Ella lately. She may be the one to ask. That is, when Brianna's not around. Without her crowd, she really is okay. She had told me how impressed she was with Kit and his abilities. She even thanked me for saving her from getting in trouble. Yeah, she's nice. And to top it off, I think she has a pretty good sense of humor. She made up a funny poem about the principal the other day, and everybody laughed.

I hadn't seen Trevor or Matt since that day at the park. I was wondering when they wanted to check out my drone. That would be fun. But I certainly wasn't going to go knocking on their door. Especially lately, as every day after school Matt seems to have his football friends over. From what it sounds like, and I hear them talking out in front, Matt's one of the captains. I'm not at all interested in football, or any sport for that matter. But to my horror, Mark noticed the football activity going on next door and got excited. He proudly mentioned that his brother played in high school. And was the star of course. And that maybe instead of soccer, he and I could go to one of their football games some time this year. Right. How about the twelfth of never.

Chapter 11

Sunday morning, I woke up hearing whistling sounds and branches banging against my window. It must have been really windy. Oh well. It's too bad because that meant I couldn't fly my drone. I didn't want to take a chance of it being swept away. Of course, all the wind sounds scared Kit, and he was hiding under my desk in the corner. I was thinking about getting out of bed. I remember Mom and Mark telling me that they had a big day, and that they'd be gone most of the afternoon. Music to my ears. And not the kind Mark listens to. They said they had lots of errands, and I think he was helping her set up a sales booth. I thought that maybe I'd just stay in bed until they left. Or maybe I'd go down and have Mom make me breakfast. I know that sounds a little spoiled and selfish, but things usually taste better when she makes them.

After I plugged in my phone to charge it, I headed downstairs in my pajamas and fed Kit. Sure enough, Mom offered to make me something to eat. She was already dressed and said they'd be leaving soon. She then asked me what I had going on today. What a stupid question. What did she think I was going to do besides play with Kit, do homework, and read? But instead of saying that, I cleverly answered, "Well, first I'm going to the symphony, then the ballet, and then off to the zoo before meeting all my new friends for happy hour."

She didn't think that was funny and called me a wise guy. But after that response, she didn't ask me any more questions, so it worked. I finished eating as Mark came stumbling down the stairs and broke two fingernails as he scooped up his keys that had dropped on the floor. They then said goodbye, slammed the front door, and left. I smiled, took a deep breath, got a book, and jumped on the sofa. Kit fell asleep next to me.

Hours passed peacefully until I heard some strange shouting from next door. I thought it was Matt's voice. The calling continued, so I got up to investigate. Which meant I poked my head out the front door. Matt was out front with two of his friends, and they were calling Trevor's name. They didn't notice me, and I was about to go back into the house, but then I saw Matt's face. Something must have been really wrong. He looked panic-stricken. I ran upstairs and threw on the nearest thing to wear—sweat pants and a long-sleeve T-shirt that I had left hanging over my desk chair. I hurried downstairs and opened my front door. They were still out there planning something. I took a few steps towards them.

"Matt, is there a problem?" I asked a bit sheepishly. He turned and faced me. He could see I was concerned.

"Yes, Kat. There is. I can't find Trevor!" Then he turned back to his friends. "Let's split up." He pointed. "Justin, you go that way. And Eric, you check with the neighbors down that way." With that command, one of the boys took off down the street calling Trevor's name, and the other one crossed the street and approached a house.

I went up to Matt just as he was deciding what to do. I could tell he wasn't sure where to begin because he was looking at the ground, shaking his head, and running his hands through his hair. Through his very pretty hair, I might add. I decided to speak up. "Where are your parents?"

He snapped out of it and turned to me again. And talked very quickly. "My dad is out of town, on a business trip. And my mom drove to the mountains and is having a big spa day with her friends. Don't know when she'll be home. I promised I'd watch Trevor all day. And I thought he was watching TV in the den while I was with the guys in the kitchen. When Justin went to leave, he told me the front door was open."

I nodded my head. "It's really windy. I bet it blew open."

"Yeah, but where would he go? I gotta find him," he said. With that, he started down the street in the opposite direction his friends went. I called out, "Matt, can I help?" He stopped and looked back. "Remember, we've had training. Kit is really good at finding things."

He looked like he was listening, so I continued.

"Kit's scent training could help. You've witnessed us in action."

"But could he find people?" he asked desperately.

"Yes. Kit and I play hide-and-seek all the time. We could use all our skills to try to find Trevor."

Now he rushed back to me. "Okay, worth a try. What do you need?"

"Go get some of Trevor's clothing. Not clean, something he's worn. Kit can pick up the scent from that. I'll go get Kit and be right out."

Matt went into his house, and I went to get Kit. But first I ran upstairs to put on sneakers. I remembered to get some treats as well as some water bottles. I shoved everything in my smaller daypack on top of my sweatshirt. That's the backpack I take on our walks. It also has a portable water dish for Kit in it, my sunglasses, and an extra house key. As I was putting Kit's leash on, I remembered that my phone was still charging, but I didn't want to have to run back upstairs and get it. I figured no big deal, Matt would have his phone, and time was of the essence.

As I was closing our front door, I started thinking about the latest Sherlock Holmes mystery I had just finished. It was called "The Adventure of the Missing Three-Quarter." Holmes and Watson used a scent hound to find a missing rugby star, who played the three-quarter position on the team. Today in rugby, they call that position a "back," but in the early days it was called the three-quarter position. In the book, the team was afraid that they couldn't win the important game against Oxford coming up unless he was found...

Matt's anxious voice slapped me back to reality. "Come on, Kat," he called out. He was already outside waiting. "We gotta hurry. Here are some socks from his hamper. Will that work?"

"Perfectly," I answered as I took them from him. Matt watched as I told Kit to sit. Then I put a sock up to his nose, gave him a few seconds to smell it, and then I said, "Kit, *search*!"

Kit looked at me, sniffed the ground, and then we took off up the street. We were walking briskly with Matt following on my right. When Matt reached for his phone, I turned to Kit and whispered, "You can do this, big guy. Find Trevor. He may be in trouble."

Chapter 12

As if Kit understood, he immediately picked up his pace. After a short while he pulled me to cross the street. He then led us up a path between two houses. Suddenly he stopped and sat. I wasn't sure why.

"Why is he stopping? There's nothing here," asked Matt as he was texting somebody.

I really didn't know. All I could do was shake my head and hope nothing was wrong. I looked down at Kit, and he wouldn't move. A moment later, as I looked up, three skunks passed across the path ahead of us. It looked like a mommy with her two babies. Momma skunk stopped and looked at us boldly. Matt and I looked back and didn't move. I wanted to tell her that we wouldn't hurt her babies, but I just smiled stupidly and tried to look like a nice person instead. Maybe that worked, because after a tense moment they all marched on.

I turned to Matt. "I don't know about you, but I'm glad Kit stopped."

Matt agreed. "Yeah, right. We don't need to get skunked right now."

When the little family disappeared into the brush, Kit rose and resumed his trot. As I looked around, I started to think that maybe we were going towards the park. But it wasn't the part of the park I was familiar with.

Kit kept sniffing, and Matt kept calling Trevor's name. No response. We kept heading in the same direction for several minutes. Suddenly, we turned and took another trail. Maybe we weren't going to the park. This path was narrow, uphill, and a little wet and muddy. And there were lots of low-hanging trees around us. At times, Matt had to bend down to avoid some of the branches. I think he bumped his head and scratched his arms a little, but he didn't complain. Probably because he felt so guilty about not watching Trevor the way he should have.

We mostly walked in silence. There wasn't much to say. It seemed like an okay time to ask him if he knew any strange news about my stupid new house. Just as I was about to ask him, he must have gotten a message because he eagerly took his phone out of his pocket. Then he looked disappointed and said to me, "Justin and Eric aren't having any luck either." I could tell he was really getting frustrated and, because he wasn't looking where he was going, he banged his head on a tree.

That must have been the straw that broke the camel's back, as my mother would say. Now he started shouting. And yelling. And then he picked up a dead branch and started hitting the tree with it. I suppose it's not important to report what words he was saying while he was clobbering the poor tree, but let's just say it wasn't the sort of conversation ladies have while sipping high tea.

And it certainly wasn't time to bug him with questions. He didn't seem to be in the mood for small talk.

He had just finished his last whack when something long and wiggly dropped from one of the branches at Matt's feet. Eek! It was a snake! And it surprised and freaked both of us out. I gasped and jumped back, but Matt shrieked and fell sideways into some mud. Out of the corner of my eye, I saw his phone fly out of his hand and land in a pool of disgusting-looking water. But he didn't notice. He was looking at the big snake.

The snake edged a little closer, picked up its head, hissed, and glared at Matt. I'd like to say that I jumped into action, shouted, threw a rock at it, or something, but I was completely paralyzed. To be honest, between you and me, I'm not really the hero type. I sadly learned this about myself when Caroline's little sister fell into a hot tub several years ago at a birthday party. I just stared at her while two other kids leaped in to save her. But that's another story. And one I rarely share. But unlike me, Kit did jump into action. He slowly approached the snake, showed his teeth, and growled. And you know what? The snake stopped, stared at Kit for a moment, lowered its head, and slithered away.

By his expression, I could tell that Matt was stunned and impressed. And I was surprised and quite proud. And happy to know that I didn't have to add snakes or mud to my always expanding list of things that Kit is afraid of. Matt got up, and we both breathed a sigh of relief. Actually, I wanted to laugh, as he was all covered with mud and looked funny, but I didn't think that would be such a good thing to do.

"Well thanks, Kit. Man, that was a close one," Matt said as he tried to brush himself off as best as he could. I could tell he was embarrassed, because he was suddenly speaking in a very low, manly voice. He then reached down, petted Kit on the head, and grumbled, "I wonder what else can go wrong today." I didn't have the heart to say it, so I just pointed in the direction of his phone, which was stuck in the bottom of the muddy puddle.

"That's just perfect," he growled as he saw it. I was hoping he wouldn't start yelling again. Thankfully, instead he just angrily picked up his phone and started to use his shirt to clean it up. It looked very wet and gooey. I hoped it was still working, but it didn't look so good.

I glanced at Kit, who seemed ready to go. So we continued to march ahead. Again, we were walking in silence. For a second I wondered if I could ask him what he knew about my house. But, even though I was dying to ask, I realized the timing again wasn't right. We needed to concentrate on the job at hand.

Finally, Matt broke the silence. "This is out of the way and too far, Kat! I don't really think Trevor would be able to come all the way here." He was very anxious. "Maybe we should go back and check with the guys. And I guess I better call my mom."

Then I remembered that having mud around might not be such a bad thing. Maybe Trevor left some visible tracks in the mud if he came this way. Looking for footprints isn't uncommon when they track criminals in my crime books. So, while Kit was attempting to pick up a scent, I let my eyes wander all along the pathway. And then I spotted something. Next to the base of a tall, scratchy bush was something that reflected the sunlight. I told Kit to sit and stay. I dropped the leash and headed to the bush. I bent over, picked it up, and noticed it was a key chain. No footprints nearby, but a pretty key chain. With two keys attached to the ring and the initials CG on a dangling colorful charm. I showed it to Matt, hoping it was Trevor's. He looked and shook his head no. But I thought to myself, *Hey, maybe I'll post it online later.* So I zipped it in my backpack.

At that point, we were all getting thirsty. Matt was grateful as I handed him a bottle of water. I had a few sips and then poured some of mine into the collapsible water dish I had for Kit. He was grateful too. Matt kept following us, but I could tell he was losing hope.

After that short break, Kit kept confidently walking us straight down the path. But I decided to focus my eyes on the ground. Two can play at this game. And I'm glad I did. I noticed that on the left was more mud. And as we were walking by, I thought I saw an impression. *It could be a little footprint!*

"Hold on, Matt. Take Kit's leash. I think I see something." Matt and Kit stopped walking as I veered to the left towards that muddy area. I carefully looked down and determined that it was a footprint! And there were several other footprints going in the same direction. After about five little steps, the mud stopped, and it became a hard dirt path again. And what I was pretty sure were footprints were no longer visible. Going back and leaning down towards the mud like Sherlock Holmes would do, I examined a print more closely. It did look like a shoe print. And it was round, and the bottom seemed smooth.

And I noticed that they were small and that the prints weren't spaced very far apart. Some clues! First, the size told me that it could be a child's. And the smooth sole told me it could be a sneaker. And then I remembered something very important. Kids take smaller steps than adults, and these footprints weren't spaced very far apart. So I came to the conclusion, or should I say brilliant deduction, that a child, possibly wearing sneakers, had been here recently.

"Matt, come here, quick," I called. He came running over with Kit. "Look at these impressions in the mud. Was Trevor wearing sneakers today?"

Matt looked down at the mud. "Yes. Always." He knelt down also and studied one of the shoe prints. "Wow, these could be his shoes. They look small and skinny. Trevor has a really narrow foot." He stood up tall. "Maybe he's nearby!" Matt looked alive again and started calling his name. He handed me Kit's leash. The moment I had the leash in my hand I gave Kit a pat on the back, and he took off again. He then made a left turn and pulled me up a slope again. Boy, I was glad we had that water break.

Soon the trees thinned out, and we walked down a hill. After a few minutes, we saw a flat, grassy area up ahead. We were approaching the park. This certainly was a roundabout way to get to the park. We went up and down and sideways to get there. And I realized we were at the part of the park I promised my mom I wouldn't go near. Oh well, sorry, Mom. What was I going to do?

Meanwhile, Matt was fiddling with his phone. I guess trying to make a call. "Great," he mumbled. "This stupid thing isn't working."

As that fact registered with Matt, he became really mad again. He picked up a big rock and threw it down the path. Quite a temper this guy has. Anyway, it hit a dirt mound and bounced off. Kit froze in his tracks and sat. We soon found out why. We heard a loud humming sound, and bees started rising from the ground.

Matt and I looked at each other with wide eyes. In front of us was a yellow cloud swarming and rushing towards us in a fury. We turned away and ran. I don't think my legs have ever moved that fast. Kit and I dashed up a trail for a minute and then hid in the brush. We crouched down very low. "It's okay, Kit. Don't be scared," I whispered as I stroked him over and over. The truth is, I was terrified. I had never been stung before, and that certainly wasn't on my bucket list. Petting Kit kept me calm. But then I heard buzzing near my ear. I stopped petting Kit and froze. I thought I felt something on my arm. I and looked down, and, to my horror, saw not one, but several bees perched on my arm. I wanted to scream and pull my arm away. But I fought the urge. Boy, was I happy to be wearing long sleeves! It was just luck that I was wearing this shirt. Usually, I wear a short-sleeve top in fall, but this one had been in easy reach. I focused on doing Mom's slow yoga breathing. Whoever thought that would come in handy? After a few seconds, which felt like an hour, they flew away. I was in the clear. I took a look at Kit, who was sitting and staring at me. He looked totally fine, which was a relief.

Kit and I stayed very still and listened for the humming of the bees. Nothing. Phew. After a few more seconds of silence, we slowly came out of the bushes and called

Matt's name. He answered and came towards us. Oops. I noticed that he had a little more mud on him, and his pants were torn in a few places. I guess he got caught up on some branches. He was wearing a short-sleeve T-shirt, and he had some red spots on his arms. Wow, Matt was really starting to look beat up. We waited quietly for a few minutes. When we felt we were safe, Matt turned to me and whispered, "Wow! I'm an idiot. I hit that cone-shaped thing with the rock. It was a bees' nest in the ground. I got a couple of stings on my arms, but I guess I'm lucky. We could have had thousands." He looked at the red bumps starting to swell on his arms. "I deserved this. Just glad I'm not allergic." His voice then cracked. "I don't think Trevor is either, but Kat, I'm so worried! Please, we gotta find him...fast!" He looked away, and I thought I heard him softly whimper.

Honestly, after all this, I was getting very worried too. But I decided to be positive like my mother would be and put my trust in Kit's abilities. I pulled Kit to get going, but of course, we carefully took another way around the bees until it was safe to return to the path. Kit then yanked my arm to the side and pulled me towards something stuck in a hedge. As I got closer, it looked like a hat. It was! A blue baseball cap. I picked it up and waved it at Matt. He came running.

"This is Trevor's!" he shouted. "He's been here. Man, I hope he's okay!" He grabbed the hat and shoved it into his back pocket. "Come on Kit, please find him." Matt brushed tears from his eyes.

I pretended not to see. I thought that after all that had happened, I'd let him have a little dignity. I quickly stated, "Don't worry, Matt. We'll find him really soon." But to be honest, I was pretty nervous. There were a lot of dangers out here for a little kid.

Chapter 13

As if Kit understood the seriousness of the situation, he quickly pulled us down the hill, onto a path, and into the park. And, sure enough, there was the group of homeless people hanging out that Mom had told me about. They had poles, tents, and cardboard boxes all set up. Kit headed right to them. Great. Now we were really heading out of my comfort zone. Besides makeshift tents, there were some sleeping bags, something that looked like a little outdoor grill, a couple of shopping carts, trash bags, a radio on a big box, and some blankets. One man was talking to himself, and a couple of people looked like they were sleeping.

Matt and I looked at each other as Kit led us right to one of the tents. He then barked and sat. What was this about? After a moment, an old man peeked out.

"What do ya want?" he growled. "Are you the police?" He had long, bushy gray hair, a big beard, and a scowl on his face. Not exactly the grandfather type you see on television.

Matt didn't back down from this old buzzard and actually stood up taller. "No, we're not the police. We are looking for my little brother. And I think he came by here."

The man thought for a second and then smiled with the few teeth he had left. He disappeared into his tent. Matt and I looked at each other, not knowing what to do. Kit was still sitting there calmly. Slowly, the old man came out, leaning on a cane and eating a donut. He had another one squished in his hand.

"These are real good today. Bobby just got back from the bakery in town." He now seemed much more pleasant as he took a big bite. "Every day they give us their old bread or donuts before they throw them out." We stared at him, unsure how to respond. He continued. "They'd rather give us their old food than have us going through their garbage in front of the customers." He chuckled. "Want one?" He held the scrunched donut out towards us with a filthy hand.

Kit seemed interested, but we both shook our heads no. Honestly, I'd rather eat a live mouse than take that donut from his hand. But I suppose it was nice of him to offer.

When he saw we weren't interested, he shrugged, popped the donut in his mouth, then reached back into his tent and came out with another one. As he was chewing with his mouth wide open, visions of Mark came to mind. I shook my head to clear it. "So who are you looking for again?" he mumbled as sugar fell onto his beard.

I didn't respond. I was too busy staring at this man's sugary beard. Thankfully, Matt took charge. "My little brother. He's five. And has brown hair and hazel eyes,"

he stated much too loudly. Maybe Matt thought that eating donuts all day affects your hearing. The man quickly nodded his head.

"Yep. I've seen him. He was here for quite a while. Nice little kid. He was lost and crying that he lost his hat. And hurtin' pretty bad 'cause his arms were all scratched up." He took another bite, and I looked away.

"Where is he now?" asked Matt anxiously.

"He said he was following a rabbit, but then he got lost. He was hungry too. But don't worry, I gave him some donuts and tended to his arms. I didn't want them to get infected. And I looked around for his hat but couldn't find it, so I gave him one of mine. He stopped crying then." He paused to take another bite. "Actually, I gave him my favorite hat."

And I'm sure Trevor looks very dapper in it, I thought to myself.

"Thanks, but where is he?" pressed Matt. Another pause.

The old man slowly continued. "He liked the sprinkle donuts the best. In fact he ate most of them except this one here." He stopped to eat again and smiled.

Matt firmly repeated, "Thank you very much for helping him. But where is he?"

"Oh, you're very welcome. Yep, he rested a while and then was going to wander off. He said his brother would be looking for him. That's when Jimmy came by."

"Who's Jimmy?" we both asked.

"He's a guy here. Nice guy. He's been here for some time now. I asked him to take the boy over to the swings.

I thought maybe he'd know some kids over there. They only left here a little while ago."

So now Trevor was with Jimmy somewhere in the park? This was only getting worse. I turned to Matt, but he had already taken off running. I guess he knew where the swings were. I did too because we often walk by them. Kit jumped forward, but I held him back. My feet were killing me. No way I could run anywhere. Except maybe to the nearest foot spa.

I muttered thank you to the donut man and set off as fast as I could. Which certainly wasn't very. But the thought of finally finding Trevor made my legs somehow move back and forth. Mark would probably tell me that if I played soccer, I'd be in better shape. And you know what? He'd probably be right. But good luck with that.

Kit and I plodded towards the swings area. The sun was going down, and there weren't that many people left in the park. When I was able to see the swings, my heart sank because no one was there. I almost felt like crying. But Kit then barked and pulled me to the left.

Instead of crying, I walked a little further and then, hooray! I finally saw them up ahead. Relief! Trevor was on a slide, and Matt was watching him and clapping. I was thrilled. There was another guy standing there watching them also.

When Trevor came down the slide, Matt caught him, and they fell to the ground laughing. As I approached, I noticed there was something odd covering Trevor's arms. I yelled to them and waved. They looked over at me, smiled, and waved back. I then took that opportunity to bend down, hug Kit, and tell him how proud I was of him.

"We got him, Kat! And he's okay!" shouted Matt.

Trevor waved again, and I noticed he had a black fedora hat on his head that fell down almost to his nose. I watched as Matt pulled it off and took the blue baseball cap out of his back pocket. Trevor grabbed it and screamed with joy.

"Matt, you found it! Yay! Jimmy, can you please give Arnie his hat back? I don't need it anymore."

The guy named Jimmy reached out and took the hat from him. Jimmy seemed like a regular, friendly guy. Sure, he was barefoot, his pants were stained, and it looked like he hadn't cut his hair in years. But he also had the biggest green eyes I've ever seen, which sparkled when he smiled. When he was Matt's age, I bet he was very good looking.

As I got closer I said, "Hi, Trevor. I'm so happy to see you."

"Hi, Kat," he answered sweetly. "I was playing here waiting for Matt. I knew he'd come and get me." Matt and I glanced at each other with a knowing look. And then he added, "Hi, Kit!" And he came over to pet him.

Once Trevor was near me, I could see that he really did have something bulky and bizarre wrapped around his arms. Were they newspapers? And mud?

"Trevor?" I asked innocently. "What's all over your arms?" Being exhausted and unsure what the answer would be, I collapsed on the grass near Matt. Trevor sat down again.

"Medicine," he answered happily. "It's medicine and bandages for my sores."

Jimmy, who was observing, spoke up with a deep voice. "Yeah. His arms were scratched up and hurting him a lot. Arnie made a paste of dandelion sap and mud. The paper is just there to hold it on."

Did I just hear that right? Dandelion sap and mud? To cover the possibility that my face might register horror, I looked down, opened my daypack, and pulled out the water bottles. I handed one to Matt, who gladly took it from me.

Trevor smiled. "And it works. My arms don't hurt as bad.

"And this medicine didn't sting like the stuff Mom puts on me." Then he looked at Matt curiously. "Did Arnie fix you up too?"

We laughed. "No, Trev," Matt answered. "This is just mud, not medicine. I slipped and fell. But maybe I should ask Arnie to cure my bee stings." He looked at me, and we cracked up again.

I guess Matt realized from the look on my face that I wasn't quite sold on this alternative medicine concoction, because he added, "Don't worry about it, Kat. It's an old survival technique. I learned about it in the Boy Scouts. We were told that dandelions are a natural herbal antiseptic and to look for them in the woods if you have a wound. You mix the sap with mud. I think people from India discovered it and still use it for natural healing."

Wait a minute. This beneficial healing solution was discovered in India? I thought of my mother's passion for yoga, which also came from India. I silently bowed my head and thanked Mom for never covering my skinned knees with this remedy before sending me to school. Matt gave Trevor his water, and he gulped it eagerly.

Jimmy stood there, staring at us as we all sat on the grass. I smiled at him, but he didn't seem to notice. It was a little strange. I guess he was deep in thought. Who knows. And who am I to judge? He was really good to Trevor.

I gave some of my water to Kit, and I slipped him a few treats. He plopped down next to me. Suddenly, Jimmy seemed to snap out of it. He looked around, put his hands in his pants pocket, and turned to leave.

Matt sat up and addressed him with respect. "Hey. Thank you, sir, for helping my brother."

Jimmy looked at Matt and murmured, "No problem. He's a good kid." As he smiled, I noticed his glistening eyes looked sad. I also noticed that, unlike the donut man, whose name I learned was Arnie, Jimmy had a nice full set of teeth.

As he started walking away, Trevor spoke up. "Thanks, Jimmy. I'll come visit you soon."

"Take care, little man," he muttered.

When he had walked far enough away, Trevor whispered to Matt, "Did you know that he lives here? In the park?"

Matt thought about it. "Yes, Trev. It's sad. Some people don't have real houses to live in like you and me. But, it doesn't mean they're strange or bad people. I'm sure everyone here has a story. You can't tell what they're like just by looking at them."

Trevor thought for a minute. "I told him I thought it would be neat to live in the park. But he said that it wasn't fun to be homeless."

With that, Matt got up and said, "Trevor, it's getting late. Let's get you home." We all got up slowly as Matt asked Trevor, "Buddy, why did you take such a long, complicated way to get to the park?

"I wasn't going to the park, Matt. I was following Mr. Pickles," he answered.

"You saw Mr. Pickles?" Matt asked curiously.

"Yes. When the front door blew open I thought I'd get the mail for Mom. And when I went outside, I saw Mr. Pickles eating a flower across the street. I called to him, but he didn't hear and ran away from me. So I followed him. I love Mr. Pickles. I wanted to catch him and bring him home."

Matt looked at him. "Are you sure it was Mr. Pickles?" Trevor nodded his head yes.

"I'm tired, Matt," Trevor whispered softly and put his hands up to be carried. That looked like a very good idea.

"What color was Mr. Pickles?" Matt asked while he was swinging him up on his shoulders.

"Brown. He's brown now," answered Trevor as we started walking.

"Maybe it wasn't Mr. Pickles," Matt said gently. "Mr. Pickles was white, you know."

"I know that," Trevor replied. "But he's been gone for a few weeks and is homeless. So he's darker now. Dirty like Jimmy and Arnie. And you."

Matt gave a little laughed and shrugged. "All right. Let's go home and get cleaned up."

"Okay, I'll get cleaned up. But promise me you won't touch my medicine and bandages," Trevor said adamantly.

Matt and I looked at each other and smiled. If he kept that promise, I wouldn't want to be there when their mom got home. We headed out the parking lot, this time taking the direct route home. It was nice to walk on the sidewalks for a change.

Chapter 14

Thankfully, the walk home from the park took much less time than the long, meandering route we took getting there. In math, I learned that the shortest distance between two points is a straight line. After my adventure, I really understood what that meant. Also, unlike when we started this journey, we were happy. Although I was beyond exhausted and getting hungry. Matt didn't seem tired, but I could tell Trevor was. Matt kept whistling and bouncing him on top of his shoulders. I was a bit envious, as my feet were screaming, *Get off of me*. Obviously, Matt was in better shape than I was. Though I noticed that the red spots on his arms were turning into welts.

Matt and I didn't talk much when we first left the park, as he was talking to Trevor and asking him questions. He wanted to hear everything that happened and all about the homeless guys who helped him. He was relieved to hear that everybody was nice and that they really were helpful. I didn't want to pipe up that my mother thinks they're dangerous and gave me a strict warning to keep away from them. From my observation, they seemed like okay people. Just guys with an alternative lifestyle, so to speak.

After it was obvious that Trevor was tired of the interrogation, Matt started talking to me. He asked me things like where I lived before and if I liked living here. He acted like he was interested. I told him a little about my life, not that it's that exciting. I did share with him that I wasn't happy being here. I said the girls are mean. He told me to give it time and that most of the people are pretty nice.

It finally felt right to ask him if he knew anything about the rumors surrounding my house. He nodded yes and started to speak up but then looked at Trevor and stopped.

"Hey, not now," he said while motioning his head towards Trevor. "Some other time." Oh darn it! Not wanting to talk about it in front of Trevor made me think this thing was even bigger than I had dreamed. I was officially dying to find out what everybody else knew except me. I wanted to say that I could cover Trevor's ears, but I came to my senses. Once again, I had to use that slow, deep yoga breath Mom taught me to calm down. It did seem to work. After that, we walked most of the way in silence.

Finally, we reached our street. In the distance, I saw his two friends sitting on his front lawn. When they saw us, they came running. That made Kit and me uncomfortable, so we hung back a little.

"Matt! Hey man, you found Trevor. Where was he?" one of them shouted as they reached us. "We couldn't get in touch with you, and we've been out there breaking our butts." One of them looked Matt and Trevor over. "And it looks like you guys have just been playing in the mud."

Matt laughed and carefully took Trevor down from his shoulders and held his hand.

As they looked at Trevor they both made faces. "What's all over Trevor's arms?"

"I'll tell you later. Trevor's fine. And thanks, guys. My phone died, and I couldn't reach you." He took it out of his pocket and showed it to them. "It's really muddy and might be too wet to ever work again."

One of the guys said, "No problem. I can fix it. I'll clean it up and put it in rice." He took the phone, and Matt nodded appreciatively.

At this point both guys were looking at me, wondering why I was there. So I put my head down and figured I'd just slink on home.

"This is Kat, my neighbor," Matt announced just as I was passing by.

One of them smirked. "And her funny-looking dog. Matt, go get Speedy out here to scare the big chicken. After today we need a good laugh." Upon hearing that, I picked up my pace towards my house.

Matt turned on them angrily, "Shut up, Justin. Kat, come back!"

I stopped. Still holding Trevor's hand, he came over and took my arm.

"Don't listen to them. You and Kit were amazing. I have you both to thank for bringing Trevor home! I don't know what I would have done without you." He looked at his friends. "You guys have to know that." With that statement both of his friends looked surprised.

"They did what?" Justin asked.

"Yes," Matt replied. "And never call that dog names again. He's very smart. And not so wimpy. He scared away a snake that was going to bite me." They both had shocked looks on their faces.

Matt continued. "Kat has taught this dog search and rescue stuff, and he's the one who found Trevor. I gave him one of Trevor's socks. He smelled it, picked up his scent, and led us to him. I'd still be out looking if it weren't for them."

There was a moment of silence.

Matt continued. "I owe a lot to Kit and Kat. They didn't have to help me. So show them a little respect."

Matt released my arm. Both boys looked at me in awe. I was embarrassed and just wanted to get home, but they came closer. I think it was Eric who said, "Wow, way to go, dog. And thanks, Kat! Hey, why don't you come to our next football game, and we'll give you a shout out."

Justin agreed and added, "And if we win, which we will, we'll give you the ball." He came over and slapped me on the back. As I almost fell forward on the pavement from that friendly smack, I thought to myself, *Why do I want a football?* Matt smiled but noticed that I looked a little confused. "Kat, that's a real honor, you know," he announced proudly.

I just stood there looking stupid, trying to recover my balance. Thankfully I thought to mutter, "Okay." And then I brilliantly added, "See ya."

As Kit and I started up the stairs to our front door, Matt shouted, "Come next Saturday. And bring Kit!"

Chapter 15

Go to a football game? I didn't even understand football.
And that means I'd have to tell Mark because of course
he'd want to come. What fun. Oh well, I didn't want to
think about that. I just wanted to take my shoes off, get
inside, and feed Kit. I reached into the zippered portion of
my daypack to grab my keys. To my surprise, I pulled out
the pretty key chain I found on that muddy path. When I
looked at the keys attached, I thought to myself how one
of them really looked like my house key. Hmmm. Same
size, same shape. Maybe most house keys look the same.
I reached in again and pulled out my house key. Don't
ask why, but for some reason, I compared them. They
really did look the same. Just for fun I put the found key
in our door. Wow, it fit. I jiggled it, and the lock turned!
Then I pushed the door, and it opened. What? Too weird!
Did the person who lost their keys live in my house? This
was all getting spooky. I stood there trying to analyze
what all this meant when Kit barked loudly, breaking
my trance. He wanted dinner. And I remembered that

I was hungry too. I shoved the keys back into my pack and left my muddy shoes outside. I decided that I would think about all that later.

When I entered, I was relieved to see that Mom and Mark still weren't home. I really didn't want to deal with them. I was hungry, thirsty, and tired. I quickly fed Kit and grabbed a banana and a couple pieces of leftover chicken. I washed my hands and then, over the sink, gobbled everything up. I found a big bag of vegetable chips with sea salt in the cupboard and took them upstairs. Kit likes these too. Before opening the bag, though, I wanted to take a hot shower. I felt all grimy and disgusting.

After a long shower, I put on my pajamas. Yeah, I know it was early, but I was tired and achy and just wanted to get into bed. I did, and it was wonderful. Unfortunately, I discovered that I had some itchy mosquito bites. That was annoying. But I realized things could have been worse as I pictured what Matt must have been going through. I softly turned on the television and ate the whole bag of chips. Of course, I remembered to give Kit the sweet potato ones. I was so relaxed and peaceful. I had lots to think about, but I didn't want to use my brain. It was glorious. But of course, just as I was drifting off to sleep, I heard Mark's voice. Which you know could wake the dead. And then I heard Mom marching up the stairs calling my name. She stared at me when she entered into my room.

"Kat, you haven't even gotten dressed today," she stated with concern. "What are you doing still in bed? Are you sick?"

"No, Mom. Just tired. I had a very busy day. You won't believe what I did," I answered softly.

She then laughed and turned off the television. "Right. I'm not going to ask you about your busy day and fall into that trap again. You're such a wise guy. Get up and come downstairs. It's time for dinner. Don't be lazy."

Lazy? Today? "Mom, I'm not hungry. I ate some of the leftover chicken, and I'm good." Then I added sharply, "And I just want to stay up here." I didn't mean to sound so unpleasant, but I was quite insulted by her last remark.

She then approached me and said gently, "Sweetie, I'm just worried that you're under the weather."

I suppose that was reasonable, so I answered, "No, Mom, really. Don't worry. I'm not sick. Just tired."

She thought for a moment. "Okay. Then stay up here. But you'll miss dessert. The nice gentleman in the booth next to mine who sells Chinese pottery brought cookies and donuts today for everybody. Usually I don't encourage eating fried sugary snacks, but the donuts looked so yummy that I must admit, I had one. And he let me bring one home for you." She paused, looked at me, and continued in a squeaky voice, "Honey, it's a chocolate donut with rainbow sprinkles on top."

A sprinkle donut? Okay, that did make me feel sick. To stop from gagging, I turned over and closed my eyes. After a moment I heard her sigh and then skip down the stairs. Good, she was gone.

I was going to turn the television back on but changed my mind. As I was lying in bed, I started to relive my crazy day. I felt like calling Evie and telling her everything. I reached for my fully-charged cell phone but changed my mind. What would I say? She didn't know Trevor and Matt and didn't really understand my neighborhood or my nose classes. And she hadn't even met Kit yet. No, I didn't think she could visualize or understand much of this stuff. Of course she would be polite, but it would be an awkward conversation. And I couldn't call Jack. He was probably busy and wouldn't be that interested in this stuff either.

I was disappointed. I definitely wanted to share my amazing experience with somebody. I heard Mom and Mark downstairs talking. But they were happy and going on and on about their day. It wouldn't be the time to interrupt. And Mom, even if she believed me, might be angry that I visited that homeless encampment when I promised her I wouldn't. Also, if I went downstairs, I might have to look at that donut.

This was confusing. My day was incredible, and I had to share it with somebody. Kit must have felt I was a little frustrated, because he jumped on the bed and licked me. We cuddled for a few minutes while I thought everything through.

Sure enough, I got an idea. I went over to my desk and grabbed a pen and a blank notebook. At least I could talk to Kit, so I said, "Kit, I know how I can share our amazing day. I'm going to write it all down. Maybe we'll have more experiences like today, and I'll write lots of stories about our adventures. And someone will publish them, and I'll become famous," I whispered in his ear. "What do you think of that?" He lifted his head and wagged his tail.

"Okay." I started playing with my pen and muttered, "I'm going to do this the old-fashioned way. With a pen and paper. The way Sir Arthur Conan Doyle wrote Sherlock Holmes. And I'm going to start right now. What do you think of the title...Kat moves to Golden Glen?" Kit put his head down. "No? You don't like that title. I don't really either." I put the pen down and thought for another moment.

"How about...the story of Kat and the missing next-door neighbor? That describes it better, right?" Kit still kept his head down and didn't respond. He didn't seem to like that one either. "Yeah, maybe it's too long. How about Kat and her adventures in Golden Glen? Is that better?" This time Kit rolled over and looked away from me.

I smiled. "Well, I see there's a problem with that one too." I stroked his fur, thinking. "Oh. I know." I hugged him tightly. "I forgot something very important. I'm sorry." I then kissed his nose. "How about we call our book... *The Adventures of Kit and Kat.*"

Upon hearing that, to my surprise Kit lifted his head, looked at me, barked, and licked my face. "Well butter my butt and hot pot of coffee!" I declared and laughed out loud. "You like that one. Then, that's the title. Who knows, this could be the first of many books in our series."

And then I remembered that key chain I found. I jumped up, unzipped my pack, and pulled out the keys. After looking at them for a few moments, I put them in my desk drawer and eased back onto the bed.

"Kit, we also have to find out why that key fits our door and what that big mysterious secret surrounding our house is. It's all very weird." I continued to dwell on those thoughts until Kit barked and put his head back on my pillow. I smiled at him. Yes, living in Golden Glen had just gotten much more interesting. I gave Kit a quick pat, picked up my pen, and started writing.

About the **Authors**

Linda Felton Steinbaum is an award-winning, produced, and published playwright. She is a member of the Alliance of Los Angeles Playwrights, the Dramatists Guild of New York, and the Writer's Guild of America. Aside from her plays being produced in her native California, her work has been performed nationally and can be found in over 50 libraries worldwide. She has a master's degree from the University of Southern California, is an avid dog lover, and supports local no-kill animal shelters. Over the years, she has taken several scent classes with shelter dogs as a way of training and socializing them. Linda was introduced to "nose work" at The Pet Orphans, a private no-kill shelter in Los Angeles where she had been volunteering for years. After raising (and house training) her children, Carly and Glenn, she now shares her home with her husband Bruce and their rescue yellow Labrador, Rex, who is the new Lab of her life.

www.lindafsteinbaum.com

Carly Steinbaum is an attorney turned entrepreneur who loves dogs—especially big dogs—and new adventures. She received her undergraduate degree from the University of Pennsylvania and her Juris Doctorate from the University of Southern California. She was drawn to create Kit and Kat with her mother after hearing about the scent class her mother took with their beloved family dog, Biscuit. She loved the idea of being able to entertain people with fun, modern, and educational stories. In her free time, Carly enjoys exploring new restaurants, traveling, and going on hikes. She lives in Los Angeles and is an aspiring dog owner.